THE CHRISTIAN FAMILY AS A DOMESTIC CHURCH

VOLUME THREE: THE DOMESTIC CHURCH:
THE WAY TO HOLINESS AND TO A HOLY DEATH

DEDICATION OF THIS WORK TO THOSE WHO HONOUR THE HOLY FAMILY OF JESUS, MARY AND JOSEPH

This book is lovingly dedicated to all those who
honour Jesus, Mary and Joseph,
the Holy Family of Nazareth
by putting their virtues
into practice and
taking positive steps
towards the development
and promotion of family
spirituality in the world.

BLESSINGS: May the blessings of the Almighty God
rain abundantly on those who use this book profitably
and make sacrifices to present any or the three volumes
of the same book as special gifts to families of their choice
for the purpose of bringing them nearer to our merciful Father in heaven.

THE CHRISTIAN FAMILY AS A DOMESTIC CHURCH

Volume Three
The Domestic Church:
The Way to Holiness
and to a Holy Death

Sir David Osunde

ISBN 978 1 80097 024 3

10 9 8 7 6 5 4 3 2 1

Nihil Obstat: Rev. Dr Victor Onwukeme MSP, former Rector of the
National Missionary Seminary of St Paul, Gwagwalada, Abuja,
and former Superior General of the Missionary Society of St Paul
Imprimatur: † Most Rev. Ignatius Ayau Kaigama,
Archbishop of Abuja, 27 December 2020

Designed by Colette Dower
Cover photo: Members of the Pontifical Council for the Family who were
present at the World Meeting of Families in Philadelphia, in 2015.
Printed in the Republic of Ireland by SPRINT-print Ltd, Dublin

*This book is printed on paper made from the wood pulp of managed
forests. For every tree felled, at least one tree is planted, thereby
renewing natural resources.*

ENQUIRIES: For all enquiries on how to reach the Holy Family Society for the
purposes of starting a new branch in your diocese, parish, Mass centre, etc., and for
registering new members/inaugurating new branches in your domain as well as placing
orders for your spiritual tools such as Prayer books, Novena Book, Song Book, Holy
Family Society Constitutions, sacramentals, etc., please contact the National Secretariat
of the society through her email address: hfsnationalsecretariat@yahoo.com

Contents

Foreword

In the Apostolic Exhortation *Ecclesia in Africa*, no. 63, Pope St John Paul II challenged theologians in Africa to work out the theology of the Church as Family, with all the riches contained in this concept. This call gave new impetus to studies on the theological and pastoral rapprochement between the concepts of church and family. In response, many authors have offered studies and reflections dealing with the theme of the Church as the Family of God. Sir David Osunde, founder, together with his wife Dame Mary-Joan, of the Holy Family Society in Nigeria, has turned the formulation around. His attention has not been held by the theme of the Church as family. Instead, he has focused on the family as a domestic church. This resonates with the declaration of Pope Francis, in the Apostolic Exhortation *Amoris Laetitia*, that 'the Church is a family of families, constantly enriched by the lives of all those domestic churches'.[1] The present book is the third volume of a trilogy prepared by Sir Osunde, with the support of his spouse, on this topic.

This publication comes at a time of growing diffidence towards associating the concept of family with the Church. This is mainly because of the instability that the family is experiencing today,

---

[1] Pope Francis, Post-Synodal Apostolic Exhortation *Amoris Laetitia*, 87, Vatican, 2016.

especially in much of the Western world and beyond. The very foundation of the family, which is marriage, has often been made the object of interference, attempted redefinition and attacks. Different types of partnerships and cohabitations are trying to lay claim to what has been for centuries a recognised and respected institution of social life. A point of reference is the current proliferation, in various parts of the world, of single-parent families, families of divorced and remarried parents, LGBTQIA (Lesbian, Gay, Bisexual, Transgender, Queer, Intersex and Asexual) parents, and the like. As various societies grapple with the challenges posed by these new realities, many people tend to become reluctant to pair the family conceptually with the Church. Sir Osunde has remained unshaken in his conviction. With exemplary firmness in his faith, he stands by his belief that the family willed by God is a domestic church. In his reflections, he has tried to highlight the spiritual benefits that one would gain in having such a functioning domestic church. He underlines the need that the Christian should first and foremost correctly understand the purpose of his or her creation by God.

In Volumes One and Two of his reflections, the author examines the following themes respectively: *The Domestic Church and the New Evangelisation* and *The Family as a Domestic Church: Experiences From the World Meeting of Families.* In the first volume, he addresses a topic that has been the principal preoccupation of the Holy Family Society for the past twenty years and tries to elucidate the preparatory ground for the development of faith in the domestic church. In nine chapters, he presents the origins of the Holy Family Society, situates it within the wider evangelisation mission of the Church and delineates its particular mission in assisting families to return to God. In the second volume, the author presents the importance and benefits of attending the World Meeting of Families in developing and maintaining a functioning domestic church. He also shares his personal experiences, together with his spouse, at those meetings.

In this book, the third of his trilogy, the author reflects on the theme, *The Domestic Church: The Way to Holiness and to a Holy Death.*

His emphasis is on the promotion of holiness in the family. He accords a privileged space to the role of parents and grandparents in encouraging people in their household to pray more, study the Word of God more, share their experiences together, and commit themselves more to doing ordinary things in extraordinary manners, as the saints did in their own times. The author affirms that when parents, grandparents, children, grandchildren and other members of the extended family frequently come together to pray, they are greatly helped in the development of their family spirituality, since God is always present in the midst of the praying family.

More specifically, the author develops the theme of this volume in eleven chapters that highlight the various elements that are necessary in the journey of the family towards holiness. Beyond the role of the parents and grandparents, he also underlines the need to take advantage of the sacraments and sacramentals that are made available to the faithful in the Church, especially the sacraments of reconciliation and the Blessed Eucharist. One chapter, the sixth, is dedicated to the value of human life, while three (the seventh, eighth and ninth) focus on the moment of passage from this life to the next, namely, lessons about life and death, preparing for a holy death and when death knocks at the door. The author does not forget to offer due space to the role of good friends in the effective development of a domestic church. He sums up his reflections on this in Chapter Ten, while in Chapter Eleven he presents a brief review of all three volumes and a reaffirmation of the need to always stand up for evangelisation.

The author has put together in this book a variety of themes that are useful for the growth of every Christian on his or her journey of faith. The experience he has gained as a grandfather and through the Holy Family Society gives him a strong authority when he writes about the family. He cites copiously from the Bible to buttress his affirmations, and this will surely endear his thoughts in this book to many. As in the other volumes, the author has enriched this book with reflections of other renowned ecclesiastics, like that of Bishop Hilary Dachelem on the value of human life contained in the sixth chapter of this volume. There is no doubt that this book, like the other two volumes, will serve as a source of useful resource materials in homes, schools, seminaries, workshops, retreats, conferences and similar study sessions. Parents, grandparents, catechists, teachers and other formators, as well as seminarians and other students will find in it great help for their personal edification and that of those entrusted to their care. The author has offered to all of us great food for thought. So, prepare your appetite.

Newtown, Trinidad and Tobago
December 2020

† Fortunatus Nwachukwu
Titular Archbishop of Aquaviva
Apostolic Nuncio to Trinidad and Tobago
in the Caribbean and the Antilles

Preface

The new evangelisation recognises that the missionary outreach of the Church takes place in a variety of contexts. In addressing the practical challenges of the new evangelisation there must be openness to new methods and processes to engage the changed societal circumstances in many countries. The new evangelisation conceives of the task as revolving around two fundamental points, namely an emphasis on an ever deepening, personal relationship with Christ and a desire to bring others into communion with him.

The missionary dimension of the family is rooted in the sacrament of baptism, through which all are commissioned to be missionary disciples, and from which the Christian family is constituted as a 'domestic church'. *Gaudium et Spes* clarifies that the task of being a father or mother is a *munus*, a Latin word that means 'service', 'gift', 'duty', and 'office'. It is also the same word used to describe the gift and burden of offices in the Church. A *munus* is an honor to receive and a burden to bear. Pope St John Paul II further affirms that, 'As a sharer in the life and mission of the Church, which listens to the word of God with reverence and proclaims it confidently, the Christian family fulfils its prophetic role by welcoming and announcing the word of God: it thus becomes more and more each day a believing and evangelising community'.[1]

---

[1] Pope John Paul II, Apostolic Exhortation *Familiaris Consortio*, 51, Vatican, 1981.

I am, therefore, happy to introduce the third volume of Sir David Osunde's book, on the Christian Family as a Domestic Church, which is titled, *The Domestic Church: The Way to Holiness and to a Holy Death*. This volume, which is one of the author's trilogy on the domestic church, places great emphasis on the promotion of holiness within the context of the family and the need to consciously prepare for our final end.

The topics treated are meant to help Christian parents and grandparents to be alive and well to their responsibilities as they exercise their offices of motherhood and fatherhood. In the realm of the home, parents and grandparents take on a similar role to that of pastors and bishops in the broader Church. They are interpreters of the love of God to those under their care. They are, to use the phrase of Benedict XVI on the night of his election, 'co-workers in the vineyard of the Lord' – in that particular corner of his vineyard in which they and their children live. Their role as fathers and mothers is truly a *munus* not unlike that of the shepherds of the Church.

To further drive home this message, the author introduces us to certain fundamentals that should underpin the setup of the family and help families make their domestic church not only functional but also successful. They include, among others, the frequent use of the sacraments, especially the sacrament of penance and the daily efforts to grow in holiness.

Ultimately, the realisation that we are all called to be saints should inform all that we do and say at the home front. It has been said that the family is a school of richer humanity. It is one of the gateways Christ has provided to those who wish to receive the abundant life he offers. It is a means of knowing and loving the one who is the glory of God, *man fully alive*. The point of the exercise of all *munera* in the Church is living lives penetrated by the love of Christ, becoming more conformed to him, and inviting others – children, spiritual or natural – to receive him. The family, therefore, is not just an essential social support, it is above all a vehicle for evangelism.

The saying goes that death is a 'necessary end'. Without coming across as alarmist, the author cautions parents and grandparents who struggle daily attending to issues in the family and participating in Church and societal duties not to forget to prepare for a holy death. He observes that it is only when parents and grandparents sufficiently prepare for a holy death that they will find a ready welcome by the Holy Family at the end of their sojourn here on earth. This, after all, is the goal of the Christian life.

The admonition by St Alphonsus de Liguori, therefore, becomes imperative: 'It is folly not to think about death, it is a greater folly to think about death and not prepare for it'. The author quotes extensively from scripture and the Church's Magisterial documents to buttress his point and put across this all-important message.

Sir David Osunde's book is the fruit of a well lived experience as a Christian parent and grandparent, and dedicated servant in the Marriage and Family Life apostolate over the years. The book is a clarion call to all, especially Catholics, to appreciate the importance of the family as an evangelising unit in the Church and to realise that evangelisation should be the Church's top priority.

Today, more than ever, there is the need to find better ways to show everyone that the Church holds the keys to true happiness and that the best reasons for coming into the Catholic Church are also the best reasons for staying. The author has done justice to the point at issue in a quite convincing manner.

The author is to be commended for breaking down and highlighting the different roles parents and grandparents play as the chief protagonists in the domestic church. He observes with great appreciation and admiration the concern our Holy Father, Pope Francis has for the youths all over the world. Due to lack of parental guidance, many youths of today are drifting away from the faith.

Pope Francis therefore recommends that opportunities be created in our communities for the transmission of the faith. This clarion call is what the author is canvassing for and should be taken on board by all, especially the members of the Holy Family Society.

Overall, this book is an attempt at responding to the Holy Father's invitation.

This publication should be considered a required reading for all Christian families. I highly and warmly recommend it to all, and I am sure it will also come in handy as a resource material for all Christian families who are seeking to live out their vocation to marriage; are passionate about spreading the Good News as missionaries and are preparing for an everlasting union with God in heaven.

† Most Rev. Ignatius A. Kaigama,
Archbishop of Abuja
Feast of St Andrew, 2020

Review Comments/Appraisals

Comment From Bishop Matthew Hassan Kukah

The family remains the central anchor that holds life and the future for any society. Sir Osunde's book draws attention to the need for us all to answer the call to evangelisation. In these challenging times, this book illustrates the emerging and engaging role of grandparents in the transmission of the message of the gospel. In these trying times, when the faith is under siege from secular forces, this book is highly recommended for all members of the family. We owe the author a debt of gratitude for a major contribution to the family apostolate.

Bishop Matthew Hassan Kukah
Diocese of Sokoto

The Domestic Church: An Appraisal of the Transmission of Faith in the Family

1. Introduction

I came across a jocund WhatsApp post: 'The teacher of the year award 2020 goes to COVID-19: Taught us what life is about, simplicity and spirituality, plus uncertainty'.

Giving thought to what the joke wishes to capture, it is necessary to point out that *uncertainty* is the crux of the matter, because both simplicity and spirituality can be erased when certainty is not safely established. In this vein, it is expedient to say that the time in which we are is yearning for salvation. With the onset of the ravaging coronavirus, which has peaked as pandemic (rated above epidemics and plagues), and with the prospects of its perduring in a fast-moving world, facets of life have automatically adjusted to the physical demands of the time with new guidelines such as social distancing, a handwashing ritual, wearing of face masks, avoidance of people, Zoom/internet facilitated virtual meetings, etc.

Many more advances in containing the pandemic are being hatched including the trials of vaccines. The physical facilities are being used to feed the spiritual world, which has been the usual path of corporal growth of the human person, yet there is need for more spiritual programmes to be injected into the set of physical adjustments for greater fulfilment in the spiritual life of human beings in this era. Such steps are being crafted by the Holy Family Society through its leadership.

2. Media Assistance to Parents and Grandparents

The media has been used to create some spiritual bouquets like virtual participation at Holy Mass, Church association meetings, community prayers and even administration of some sacraments without observing moral distance, proximity, etc. As the physical domain keeps adjusting and inventing ways and means of containing this *distraction* in the world of our experience, the spiritual domain needs to brace up for her concerns.

Providentially, some of the *perennial distractions* in the spiritual life can receive more effective and concerted cleanup in this pandemic era and afterwards. It is possible to hand down the faith to generations yet unborn through the apostolate of parents and grandparents. In this regard, parents and grandparents should cultivate and encourage a positive attitude to the media so as to apply its positive ends in mentoring their children. The active role of parents and grandparents in evangelisation in the present day can give a great boost to the family. Parents and grandparents can no longer give the excuse that their children will receive religious instruction elsewhere outside the home.

The concerted effort with which they see their children through formal education in this COVID-19 era should be replicated in the religious training of their children too. But unlike formal education where help of experts may be imperative, the spiritual life is where parents and grandparents should be models. Parents have a greater responsibility thrust upon them in the modern era. They are not free in conscience to bear witness to a *half-truth* or to their own brand of the message of salvation but to the entire truth of revelation in Christ.

3. Church Teaching and Parental Guidance
The Church teaches that 'God has arranged that the things he had once revealed for the salvation of all peoples should remain in their entirety, throughout the ages, and be transmitted to all generations'.[1] This arrangement by God has to be fitted and suited to the age in which we are. Parents and grandparents are to bear their vocational witness to Divine Revelation. The reason that God arranged for the revelation of his salvation to be transmitted intact to all generations is

---

[1] Pope Paul VI, Dogmatic Constitution on Divine Revelation *Dei Verbum*, 7, Vatican, 1965.

because God 'desires all men to be saved and come to the knowledge of the truth' (1 Tm 2:4). And that truth is Jesus Christ (Jn 14:6).

An avenue of exploration for the effective transmission of this eternal command is the effective use of the compulsory 'stay at home' order of parents and grandparents with their children when the 'new normal' means having minimal physical contact with other families and people outside their home. Parents and grandparents are therefore meant to lead and teach by example and use words where necessary. For instance, prayers are best learned by children by joining their parents, grandparents and siblings in prayer in the home.

4. Creativity Within God's Creation

This is an era of creativity in storytelling as in the invention of teaching aids. Facilitating parents can create programmes that could be writ large in the media, spurred on by their experiment in the home. This is expected because we live in the digital era, daily reaching new crescendos in programming and re-programming events in the world.

No one can doubt the fact that we are living in an internet era on the superhighways. Technology is moving fast in many ways with regard to physical development. We can also move fast in ways of understanding God and living the faith. In the contemporary world, faith in God can be expressed in the language and grammatical terms of scientific programming. Once it is accepted that human beings are still being created by God and not by technology, there will be nothing wrong in using internet facilities to know and serve God, who is the author of who we are and what we are.

God knew us before we were born. He created our parents and grandparents through whom we came into this world. As such, we do not have any secrets before God. By the very fact of our birth, God chose us to come into existence because he loves us. The Psalmist says, 'my being held no secrets from you, when I was being formed in secret, textured in the depths of the earth. Your eyes could see my embryo. In your book all my days were inscribed, every one that was fixed is there' (Ps 139:15–16). The challenge and project before each human being is the task of knowing and loving God who first knew and loved us. This task must come into the programme of the family living in the consciousness of the presence of God in our era.

5. Setting the Goals of Spiritual Life in family

Parents and grandparents should set goals of spiritual activities for their children. Recently, I came across a saying, 'Goals without plans are mere wishes' (attributed to Antoine de Saint-Exupery, an author and poet).[2] In other words, if a person says he has goals to attain but has no plans towards attaining those goals, the person is only expressing a wish. Each individual attains the personal goals they set for themselves. The great help in attainment of personal goals includes the influence of parents and grandparents. Before it can be said that something occurs regularly in a family, the seed must be planted. This is why it can be said that something 'runs in the blood' of a family. Practice of the faith is one such thing that can appear to run in a family.

6. Parental Faith in the Upbringing of Jesus

Jesus was first presented in the temple by his parents, Mary and Joseph (Lk 2:22–39). His parents also took him to Jerusalem for the feast of Passover (Lk 2:42–43). Later in life Jesus himself was often seen in the synagogue teaching and healing. In fact, the first instance when Jesus was found in the temple was when he was yet a child under the care of his parents. While the family of Jesus, Mary and Joseph were returning from the feast of Passover when Jesus was twelve years old, the referent incident happened. His parents presumed he was with their relatives and acquaintances returning home from the feast. Three whole days had passed before they began

---

[2] *LinkedIn*, https://www.linkedin.com; accessed on 15 September 2021.

searching for him. When they did not find him, they returned to Jerusalem only to discover that Jesus had stayed back in the temple.

When they found him, Jesus made it clear that he belonged to the temple, to the temple where his parents had presented him on the day of his purification and dedicated him to God. Jesus said to his mother and the search party, 'Why were you looking for me? Do you not know that I must be in my Father's house?' (Lk 2:49).

The presentation of Christ in the temple is an example of how the action (faith) of parents can show the way to the child. The parents of Jesus not only dedicated him there, they took him to the temple to worship God. Although Jesus was God in the form of man and would fulfil all righteousness, he learned how to worship God from his parents. In his flesh as God incarnate, the parents of Jesus showed him the way to the temple. This should interest many, just as I find an interesting link between the dedication in the temple and the finding of the child Jesus in the temple. He who was dedicated to God was later found in the temple serving God to whom he was dedicated. What a great example of how to serve and worship God in spirit and in truth! The parents of Jesus dedicated him to God, and being in human form, he learned from them how to dedicate himself to God.

The parents of Jesus taught him how to pray when they took him to the temple to pray, especially during their feasts. Jesus was later seen at prayer (Lk 3:21; Lk 6:12; Jn 11:41; Mt 26:36) and he taught his disciples how to pray (Lk 11:2–4). Having been introduced into the service of God, his Father, he spent his life teaching and healing both inside and outside the temple. Interestingly, Mary, the mother of Jesus, had devout parents, Joachim and Anne, who had trusted in the Lord and dedicated her to God. They brought Mary up in the fear of the Lord. God found favour with her whom Joachim and Anne brought up in the fear of God.

7. Faith in the Blood of Timothy

Here we recall the letter of Paul to Timothy when he was encouraging him to remain faithful in the apostolate. Paul made reference to the faith of Timothy as 'sincere faith, which first dwelt in your grandmother, Lois, and in your mother, Eunice, and I am sure also in you' (2 Tm 1:5). If faith dwells in Timothy as in his grandmother and mother, would it then mean that faith runs in their biological blood? Scientifically, the answer is 'no'. Faith is not like a disease or an immunity traceable to a family lineage or as an item in their blood makeup.

In practical Christian living, faith can be passed on from one generation to another as fruits of their lives. What proves that faith is not a genetic trait is the experience that not every child of a faithful father or mother remains faithful as their parent. However, those who walk along the good path of their ancestors are said to have inherited the faith of their parents and grandparents where applicable. The faith of Timothy was traced to his mother and grandmother to highlight the good upbringing that promotes good actions, resulting from the belief in God shared in their family.

Faith is the gift of God received by a person and domesticated in life situations. Divinely inspired actions can solidify into a family culture. Faith bears fruit in good works. St James teaches that 'Faith without good works is dead' (Jas 2:17). He presented the relationship of faith and good works in such a way that good works alone show the faith of a person: 'But someone may say, so you have faith and I have good deeds? Show me this faith of yours without deeds then? It is by my deeds that I will show you my faith' (Jas 2:18).

8. Faith as Flowing in the Family Line

Jesus used so many images to convey the message of the kingdom of God/heaven. These images are vivid examples of how faith can be planted in the family. 'The kingdom of God is like a mustard seed which a man took and threw into his garden' (Lk 13:19; Mt 13:31).

The mustard seed when grown becomes the biggest of the trees. Such applies to little seeds of faith sown and nurtured in a family setting, in the fertile ground of intelligent children. The idea here is that there is need for growth, effort and progress in other to attain heaven. Again, Jesus says, 'the kingdom of God is like the yeast a woman took and mixed in with three measures of flour till it was leavened all through' (Lk 13:21). The bread leavens because the baker applies regulated fire to the mixture. Likewise, faith is to be fanned to flames in the family by parents and grandparents.

In the Gospel of Matthew, Jesus used the image of the kingdom of heaven in many parables: 'The kingdom of heaven may be compared to a man who sowed good seed in his field' (Mt 13:24–30). There, he discussed the bad seed introduced by the enemy of the kingdom. In this scenario we see the need for vigilance. Weeds represent the many *distractions* to the faith in the world. Yet, the family is special and plays a key role in one's life. Because of this, parents and grandparents are not free to disown their children but must nurture them with the patience of God typified in the farmer who waited for harvest time to sort the good from the bad fruits. Prayer can do a lot in family apostolate. The human fruit is such that before the harvest time, the wayward child of today could become a saint.

Again, Jesus told this parable, 'The kingdom of heaven is like treasure hidden in a field, which someone has found; he hides it again, goes off in his joy, sells everything he owns and buys the field' (Mt 13:44–45). Nothing is beyond the efforts required to get families on the right footing by parents and grandparents. Being a parent or grandparent entails much sacrifice for the sake of the salvation of your children. Sometimes, parents take things for granted and become the cause of scandal to their children. Such seeds once sown remain indelible, and mature to become a great disservice to the Church.

The bad examples of parents and grandparents are some of the things that can also flow in the family bloodline. Jesus repeated this idea of sacrifice in another parable: 'The kingdom of heaven is like a merchant looking for fine pearls; when he finds one of great value he goes and sells everything he owns and buys it' (Mt 13:46). The hidden treasure may appeal to agriculturists, as the fine pearls would capture the interest of those engaged in commerce.

Jesus also handled the issue of having 'good' and 'bad' children in the same home and of the same parents. Sometimes it does happen that a child from a good home appears to be a 'black sheep' in the circle. Concerning this and similar situations in life, Jesus said, 'The kingdom of heaven is like a dragnet that is cast in the sea and brings in a haul of all kinds of fish … sitting down, they collect the good ones in baskets and throw away those that are no use' (Mt 13:47–48). Parents are called to serious duty amidst good and bad children of a family.

9. Conclusion
The Holy Family Society is blazing a trail in championing the deepening of faith in the family by natural social planning, using modern means of communication and responding effectively to the demands of the time. Sir David Osunde, the author of the three volumes of this book, has studied the generic and extraneous distractions to the growth of faith in the family and has enumerated suggestions and a roadmap for ensuring growth in the right direction. As he rightly holds, the forces of darkness bombarding the family institution are the handiwork of the evil one.

The devil knows that the destabilisation of the family is the sure route to perdition in the world. A sublime way of removing the force of the family in fostering spiritual growth is by parents and grandparents not acceding to suggestions of the devil. One of the obstacles to proper parenting is the perennial excuse of having a busy schedule. Unexpectedly, the positive side effect of human beings slowing down to develop their family spirituality resulted from the lockdown in the world during the coronavirus pandemic. Many households used the opportunity to deepen the faith of their family members. Is it any wonder that the best Christian fellowship takes place in the family circle? That was how the early Church was built and humanity can do it better in our era.

Rev. Fr Cosmas Okecuchukwu Ebebe, PhD, FNPR
Lecturer, Department of Systemic Theology
Catholic Institute of West Africa
Port Harcourt, Nigeria

Acknowledgements

This acknowledgement is unmistakably my special tribute to all those who worked towards the successful completion of the three volumes of this book. Let me make it clear from the start that the input from different sources for one volume inspired the preparation of the next volume, allowing the three volumes of the book to evolve naturally and miraculously. The miraculous completion of the three volumes on the domestic church within a space of nine months came to be because with God all things are possible.

It is important to note here that the writing of this book was never planned, hence it can be attributed to a miracle – a miracle in the sense that a thought suddenly came to the author that out of the coronavirus pandemic foisted on the world, something good can also come out of it.

With such a thought, I went into a quiet corner to ruminate about what to do next. It took another week or so before the directive and the direction came my way. The reader may want to know that I left Nigeria with my wife for the United States of America in November 2019, without planning to stay more than two months. Our main purpose for the visit was to await the arrival of our twenty-fifth grandchild as our daughter, Dr Marian Imaze Davis, was heavily pregnant. We were to wait there to conduct the baby's naming ceremony and participate in its baptismal ceremony in the Catholic Church before returning home in the New Year. This was our family plan. But God had a different plan for us. Our daughter, who was expecting her sixth child, had the baby on 5 December 2019, and both the naming ceremony and the baby's baptism took place on 29 December 2019. As it was a period of several celebrations, the days seemed to have moved quite fast, and before we could shout 'Alleluia' and 'Happy New Year' at many more occasions, we found ourselves already in the middle of January 2020.

Our daughter then advised us that before thinking of hurrying back to Nigeria, we should have a thorough medical examination, advising further that we should therefore move the dates on our air tickets forward. This was exactly what we did, only to discover that a few of our medical appointments were in February, March and April 2020. And before we could attend two of the different medical appointments, the coronavirus pandemic had set in. With the medical advice about social distancing, cancelling of travel plans, wearing of masks and restriction of movements to public places, we found that we had no choice than to settle in, watch the world from America, and pray for the coronavirus pandemic to disappear so that we could return to Nigeria.

This was not to come quickly and we were left with no other choice than to spend several hours on the phone every day to speak on a number of issues to different people in various parts of the world. It was at this point that the Holy Spirit entered, questioning through the inner voice: 'Why are you not making good use of the time I have given to you?'. This woke me from my deep slumber, and I personally settled in to undertake the task of writing a few chapters of my family experiences regarding the outcome of our effective use of our domestic church.

Looking around my room, I had only the Catechism of the Catholic Church, the Holy Family Society Prayer Books, the Community Holy Bible and other prayer books for different occasions. I immediately listed other books I might need for reference purposes for my daughter and her husband, Mr Tyree T. Davis, to place an order from the Pauline Bookshop in Miami. The books included: the Revised Standard Version Bible (Second Catholic Edition), Documents of Vatican II, and the Code of Canon Law.

It was only when these arrived, that I said to myself, that it could be possible that the coronavirus pandemic, which was weekly claiming thousands of human lives might really bring about good things that would help to transform people's lives as well as bring sanctity to many. I also reasoned that my own work during the period could, with great personal sacrifices, help to bring Christian and non-Christian families nearer to God.

With such thoughts reverberating in my mind, I began to work on the first two chapters of the book based on the papers I had presented at conferences in the past. It became necessary for me to find who amongst our priests would be ready to travel the same route with me by spending quality time out of their busy schedules, to proofread and edit the scripts. After several contacts, I found a willing hand in the person of Rev. Fr Dr Victor Onwukeme, MSP, a former Rector of the Major Seminary of St Paul's Missionary Society, Gwagwalada, Abuja, and also a former Superior General of the congregation of the Missionary Society of St Paul (MSP).

His acceptance to travel the same route with me boosted my spiritual energy. I then decided to be more serious in moving from writing one chapter of the book to another. And I noticed that as I was finishing the first volume, I found that there were still many thoughts in my mind that were yet to be expressed. I felt it would be unwise to allow them to disappear.

So, I begged the Rev. Father to be kind enough to go through a second volume of the book with me, and he generously obliged without any hesitation, but made it clear to me that with several other works in his hand, I should not expect quick turn out of his proofreading.

With this settled, and knowing that the road was not clear for my wife and I to return to Nigeria, I then concentrated on the second volume, which was then planned by me to incorporate the experiences of other families in the development, promotion and functioning of their domestic churches. I created room for other families to tell their individual stories. On 6 and 7 May 2020, I sent out two notices in addition to the previous one I had sent out on 25 April 2020, requesting families to give their own testimonies on how the functioning of their domestic churches has helped them to develop their family spirituality. The message I sent out was titled:

> The Domestic Church: Why not make your family a part of the new mission on Global Family Evangelisation by giving your family testimony?

A part of the message I sent out read thus:

> A few days ago, (precisely on 25 April 2020), I intimated you through this WhatsApp platform about the intention of the Holy Family Society to put on the shelf for everyone, Christians and non-Christians alike, a new book on the domestic church as part of her efforts to impress on family members throughout the world to pay much more attention to the development of their family spirituality.
>
> This, we believe, Christians and non-Christians can do by, first and foremost, returning to their roots to make beneficial use of their homes as they organise themselves into family praying groups with a view to living the lives exemplified by the early Apostles and disciples of Christ. We also believe that some families among us already have a lot of experiences in organising their family devotions in the comfort of their homes, giving opportunities to everyone to develop themselves spiritually when they share the Word of God together, each day ...
>
> We therefore see it as a good thing for many growing families to learn from the initiatives of keen followers of Christ,

especially as regards the steps taken by them to keep their domestic churches functioning in the last ten or more years.

We will be so highly delighted to receive your genuine testimonies that we can take to the field to share joyously with others, with a view to winning more families for Christ. Meanwhile, we are praying that enlightened Christian families reading the above will happily devote quality time to prepare their own testimonies which could form part of the legacies they will happily leave behind for future generations.

The above letter went through many group WhatsApp platforms to hundreds of families. After a number of reminders and after over three months of waiting for responses, only five families responded. Their stories are quite enriching and they are now good legacies that can spur many to positive action on improving their spiritual lives. This explains why their testimonies have been given prominent places in Volumes One and Two of this book. The families who contributed their very informative and inspiring family stories include:

(1) Dr David Ezeh, An Assistant Director, currently working in the Federal Ministry of Finance, Budget, and National Planning, Abuja. His family story can be found in Volume One, Chapter Four.

(2) Mrs Georgiana Ogochukwu Ogbutor, a retired Director in the Federal Civil Service of Nigeria. Her family story is in Volume Two, Chapter Seven.

(3) Mrs Ivonne Ruiz, An American housewife and a parishioner of St Brendan's Catholic Church, Miami, Florida. Her soul-captivating story is also in Volume Two, Chapter Seven.

(4) Clemetina Osayuwamen Osunde, Manager of a Secondary School Cafeteria in UK. Her own story is published in Volume Two, Chapter Six.

(5) Dr Mrs Marian Imaze Davis, a medical practitioner, with her own private medical practice in Miami, Florida. Similarly, her family story is incorporated in Volume Two, Chapter Seven.

There is no way I can thank them enough for their valuable contributions to the two volumes of this book. I must also use this opportunity to thank my fifteen-year-old granddaughter, Miss Glenda Oloke, who accompanied her mother, Mrs Augusta Ehinoma Oloke, to be in my entourage to attend the Ninth World Meeting of Families in Dublin, Ireland. She revealed in her powerful write-up, how her experiences in Dublin have strengthened her spiritual life. This can be found in Chapter Six of Volume Two of the book. It is advisable that parents should share her captivating testimony with their children.

Before using this same forum to thank all who made inestimable contributions to the production of these three volumes of work on the domestic church, let me quickly observe here that while I was still contemplating how to fully express my additional thoughts in Volume Two of the book, I realised that within four weeks of my requesting people to send in their own stories, Pope Francis was also sending out a similar message to people to mark the Fifty-fourth World Communications Day 2020, which was held throughout the world on Sunday 24 May 2020. He used the occasion to call all Mass Communicators and Christian families alike who have enviable stories about their lives to write them as such stories can become an 'appendix' to the bible.

Reading Pope Francis' message to mark the 2020 World Communications Day really spurred me on because a good part of it coincided with my thoughts about writing our faith-building stories to open doors for us in the new crusade to evangelise families. Be that as it may, it gave me a clear indication that God is really supportive of our new initiative, as he was using different people to send out similar messages. I personally got a further spiritual push to complete

Volume Two and then moved on to put down my thoughts in Volume Three.

This is what brought about the three volumes of the work coming out at the same time. Is there any wonder that I attributed this to a miraculous undertaking and achievement? And does it also not reveal to the reader now that 'they who wait on the Lord shall renew their strength' (Is 40:31)?

Now it is time to give due honour to all who made the dream of producing the three volumes of this book on the domestic church a reality.

First and foremost, I wish to thank the almighty God for keeping all who participated in one way or the other in the production of the three volumes of this book safe and hearty during the period of the ravaging coronavirus pandemic. That I did not lose my bearing all through in my attempt to remember everything my wife and I did together to raise our children to be who they are today, I wish to give special thanks to her for being very supportive and productive.

Let me humbly state here that my wife, Dame Mary-Joan Osunde, whose activities at home, in the Church and in the community also attracted the Vatican, was considered for a Papal Honour of the Knight of St Sylvester by Pope Benedict XVI in 2005. This understandably shows that her care, loyalty and love for her husband, the Church and the community where she lives, are exemplary; I myself was similarly honoured as Papal Knight of St Sylvester by Pope St John Paul II in 1992.

Considering what the Church Magisterium majorly did to direct our course in life as well as make the three volumes of the book available on the shelves, my family and I cannot really find the appropriate words to express adequately our heartfelt gratitude to Pope Francis and other Church leaders whose works I personally used copiously to buttress the various points I made in the three volumes of this book. Nor can I find the adequate words to express my immense thanks to our Church leaders who participated physically by contributing very valuable scripts that are incorporated in the three volumes of this book.

For the reader to know what came from our spiritual leaders who encouraged me to complete this work, I wish to simply refer to what each of them did specifically below, imploring them to kindly forgive me for not consulting them first before listing their names in this acknowledgement. Those among them who found time to quickly attend to our urgent requests as we solicited for their input include:

(1) Most Rev. Dr Augustine Akubeze, President of the Catholic Bishops' Conference of Nigeria, and the Archbishop of Benin City. He wrote the Preface for Volume Two of the book and also gave the Imprimatur for the same volume.

(2) Archbishop Augustine Kasujja, Apostolic Nuncio to the Kingdom of Belgium and to the Grand Duchy of Luxembourg. He wrote the Foreword for the same Volume Two.

(3) Most Rev. Dr Ignatius I. Kaigama, immediate past President of the Catholic Bishops' Conference of Nigeria, and the Catholic Archbishop of Abuja. He wrote the Preface for Volume Three and also gave the Imprimatur for the same Volume Three.

(4) Archbishop Fortunatus Nwanchukwu, Titular Archbishop of Aquaviva, Apostolic Nuncio to Trinidad and Tobago, in the Caribbean and Antilles. He wrote the Foreword for Volume Three.

(5) Most Rev. Dr Valerian M. Okeke, Archbishop of Onitsha. He wrote the Preface for Volume One and also gave the Imprimatur for the same Volume One.

(6) Most Rev. Dr Emmanuel Adetoyese Badejo, Bishop, Catholic Diocese of Oyo. He contributed a piece for Volume Two, Chapter Three, titled: 'Catholic Teaching About a Spirit-filled Domestic Church'.

(7) Most Rev. Dr Matthew Hassan Kukah, Bishop, Catholic Diocese of Sokoto. He contributed an incisive Comment on Volume Three, which is at the beginning pages of the volume.

(8) Most Rev. Dr Jude Arogundade, Bishop, Catholic Diocese of Ondo. He wrote the Foreword for Volume One of the book.

(9) Most Rev. Dr Hilary Nanman Dachelem, Bishop, Catholic Diocese of Bauchi. He contributed a piece for Volume Three, Chapter Six, titled: 'Human Life: What Value to Attach – Does Mine Have a Meaning?'

(10) Rev. Fr Agbonkhianmeghe E. Orobator, SJ, President of the Jesuit Conference of Africa and Madagascar. He contributed a piece, titled: 'What the Church Expects of a Functioning Domestic Church'. This can be seen in Volume Two, Chapter Four of the book.

(11) Rev. Fr George Ehusani, Executive Director, Lux Terra Leadership Foundation. He wrote a Review Comment on Volume Two of the book.

(12) Rev. Fr Dr Victor Darlington, Parish Priest of Sacred Heart Catholic Church, Camberwell, SE5, 9QS, London, UK. He contributed a piece, titled: 'What the Church Expects of a Catholic Marriage'. His contribution forms part of the piece in Volume Two, Chapter One.

(13) Rev. Fr Cosmas Okechukwu Ebebe, PhD, FNPR. Lecturer, Department of Systemic Theology, Catholic Institute of West Africa, Port Harcourt, Nigeria. He did an insightful Appraisal of Volume Three of the book.

(14) Rev. Fr Oseni J. Osilama Ogunu, OMV, Dominican Institute, Ibadan and Founder/President of the Foundation for Human Rights and Development of African Christian Heritage. He wrote the Review Comment on Volume One.

(15) Rev. Fr Alexander Ekechukwu CSSp MA, University of London, England, Doctorate in Theology, Gregorian University, Rome, Italy. He wrote a comment on Volume One.

(16) Rev. Fr George Adimike, a PhD student in Rome who successfully completed his studies in Rome in 2020 and returned immediately to Nigeria to found what he described as the Faith-Inspiration Project. In spite of his mourning the death of his loving father, Chief Patrick Ndubueze Adimike, who went to his eternal reward on 11 June 2020, he still found time to help me to prepare a draft script that went out to one of our bishops.

(17) Rev. Fr John Paul Ojuikpai, Parish Priest, St Martin Catholic Church, Oso Edda, Abakaliki Diocese. He contributed a piece, requesting to be assisted in solving a marital problem in his parish in respect of a Christian who married two wives and now wants to reconcile himself with the Church for him to become once more, a communicant. His piece can be found in Volume Three, Chapter Two.

(18) Rev. Fr Osemhantie Okhueleigbe, Personal Secretary to Archbishop Patrick Ekpu, (Archbishop Emeritus of the Archdiocese of Benin City), contributed the first response to Rev. Fr John Paul Ojuikpai's request. This is also in Volume Three, Chapter Two of the book.

(19) Rev. Fr Henry Nkemakolam Emeka, Assistant Parish Priest, Christ the King Catholic Church, Magwi County, Eastern Equatorial State, South Sudan, sent in the second response regarding how to solve the problem of a polygamous husband who wants to reconcile himself with the Church and with God. His contribution is also in Volume Three, Chapter Two.

(20) As a way of giving a global look on the whole work I have completed, a Papal Knight of St Gregory the Great, Ambassador Martin Ihoeghian Uhumoibhi, OFR, KSJI, D.Phil. (Oxon), took quality time to appraise it, and he came up with a piece, titled: 'The Home as the First Congregation: An Appraisal of David Osunde's Theology of the Domestic Church'. This can be found in Volume One of the book.

There were others who read one or two volumes of the book and sent in their very inspiring comments. Their names cannot be individually mentioned here because of lack of space. Members of my family are joining me here to commend everyone to God for his special blessings. Our special commendation also goes to Rev. Fr Dr Victor Onwukeme, MSP, who made great sacrifices to proofread and edit the scripts contained in Volumes One, Two and Three of the book. I was like Oliver Twist, asking for more and more as I consumed his time with more and more work, sometimes making him read one script three times as we exchanged thoughts.

This exchange of thoughts helped a great deal in my redoing one of the chapters in Volume Three before both of us agreed that it met the standard of my previous works. For his insistence that the work be redone, I want to specially thank him for being a good teacher to me, otherwise the reader would have seen a good number of errors in this work.

In conclusion, I wish to thank all our children, grandchildren, brothers and sisters and other extended family relations who stayed in our home during their growing years for comporting themselves and adjusting to the rules in our home. It is true that some of you described it then as being in a sort of 'family military school'. But what many of you took out of the Christian home certainly impacted in you the virtues of discipline and agape love for your fellow human beings, in addition to the spiritual benefits we all shared in the home. These you should all now take along with you to affect the community where you live.

May the almighty God continue to bless the work of our hands as he directs each and every one of us, especially those who contributed immensely to the realisation of this project, to greater achievement.

Feast of St Joseph the Worker,
1 May 2020, Miami, Florida
Sir David E. Osunde
Founder/National Coordinator, Holy Family Society

1

Transmission of Faith From Grandparents to Children and Grandchildren

No one needs to be told today that there has been a continuous, widening gap in the passing of the faith of grandparents to their children and grandchildren. This has been due to a lack of seriousness and the *distractions* that have virtually enveloped the world. The resultant effect of this is that there has been a declining level of connectivity in the transmission of the Christian faith and family values from one generation to the other. This being the case, it has become much more urgent now that we do something about the current situation because of the numerous distractions and noise pollution in the world.

As this chapter is being prepared, the invasion of coronavirus on the world has caused many distractions, apart from the thousands of human lives it has claimed already. This has given an uncomfortable signal to everyone that the world will not be the same again, hence we find people now talking about the 'new normal'. In this so-called 'new normal', people are being made to rely more on virtual communications and less on interpersonal communications. Many institutions now permit their workers to work more from home these days than being at their places of work every day of the week to interact with their fellow workers in the office. Such interactions are being deemed unnecessary as people can phone each other, have a conference call through the phone or have a Zoom meeting where vital issues can be discussed and resolutions taken. Such Zoom meetings can accommodate more than twenty people and everyone who is connected is able to bare out his or her mind during the meeting.

The same is happening to those who normally attend their places of learning, from kindergarten to university level. Similarly, those who usually go to the supermarket to shop for household items, groceries and foodstuff, especially in the developed parts of the world, now depend more on ordering their supplies and have them delivered to their doorsteps. As regards going to the Church and other places of worship, people are also being made to depend more on virtual communication and online streaming of Mass, as well as other services in the Church or in the Mosque. In the same manner, a mind-boggling fear of the deadly coronavirus has been driven deeply into the hearts of the people as everyone is being discouraged through daily publications from having direct interpersonal communications with people of different walks of life. This, in effect, has stopped many from reaching out to people of faith that we normally rely on for the purpose of developing our own faith. And if anyone must carry out a visit, a social distance of six feet has to be maintained throughout their interaction.

Distractions Caused by Forces of Darkness

The worst aspect of this distraction that is caused by the forces of darkness is that apart from the loss of hundreds of thousands of lives already in the world, there has been a massive amount of socio-economic damage and ruin to employment everywhere. This has prompted many to adopt a 'sit tight' approach. All these happenings are being described as the 'new normal'. The so-called 'new normal' has affected many people in different ways, with many facing a lot of trauma.

What all this means is that it will require thousands of psychologists to speak to the hearts of many 'sitting on the fence'

Christians, Moslems, Hindus, etc., for them to be able to return to their places of regular worship after the current lockdown. With the current development, it must be understood now that apart from the psychologists that will be needed to help distressed families to come out of their dilemma, grandparents also have a lot to do now to wake up their children and grandchildren to the realities of life in the face of the pandemic. They must let their children and grandchildren know that, despite the difficulties in the land, our God remains our God. He is an unchanging God regardless of what the scientists are doing with the coronavirus, which is a human creation.

Greater Responsibilities From the 'New Normal' in Society

Knowing now that people are reluctantly, or in some cases, happily buying into the current 'new normal', grandparents and parents must realise at this point in time that it behoves them to meet the current challenges by taking on more responsibilities towards the provision of substantial spiritual, educational and material care for their children and grandchildren. There is no doubting the fact that these are huge responsibilities, which grandparents and parents cannot, in all honesty, address adequately.

But as things stand today, there is no denying the fact that the diminishing interpersonal relationship of infants, pupils and students with their caregivers, teachers and lecturers, has left a wide range of work for the grandparents and parents to carry out on a daily basis to help their children and grandchildren acquire knowledge in different areas of life. The challenge to the grandparents and parents is that the children and grandchildren are much more experienced in the computer knowledge that is seemingly dominating the world.

Be that as it may, parents and grandparents must not lose hope in directing their children and grandchildren appropriately, especially in the area of directing them back to God, who created them in his image and likeness. Children and grandchildren are to, first and foremost, learn from their parents and grandparents that whatever knowledge they acquire in this world, if it is not directed towards serving the living God, becomes useless. This is why it must be explained to them that spiritual knowledge is the most valuable of all, as it will direct them in all matters towards God.

It must also be made quite clear to them that the acquisition of knowledge in other subjects such as science, education, computers, civics, government, politics, business, etc., are not condemnable but they should be used for good purposes. If these are brought to the understanding of the children and grandchildren, it will be easier for the parents and grandparents to focus more on the spiritual development of the children and grandchildren. This can only happen when the home is set out for good spiritual development of both the old and the young in the family. Everyone in the home, including the children, should be psychologically prepared for this, especially when they are all following religiously the schedules that have been designed for all. The best meeting point in the home for everyone to congregate and interact with one another is the place that is designated for prayer or in a private chapel within the premises.

To make a good beginning in the home is to let everyone know that whatever we do in this life must be centred on Christ. This was why God himself appeared during the transfiguration of Jesus at Mount Horeb to speak to the whole world, saying: 'This is my beloved Son, with whom I am well pleased; listen to him' (Mt 17:5). So, the main duty of the grandparents and parents is to consciously lead all within their household to Jesus, as he has sufficient room in his heart for everyone who comes to him. To get everyone going in the right direction, grandparents have more of a duty to perform – to encourage and inspire all within the household to come together every day for prayer, listen attentively to the gospel message, share what each participant understands from the message and then learn how to act upon it. The experiences of elders who participate in such sharing becomes a beacon of light for those who take them to heart. This undoubtedly contributes, to a large extent, to the building of a solid foundation for the younger ones in the household.

But grandparents and/or parents who fail to do this will not only be building a weak foundation of faith for their children, grandchildren and wards, but will also, inadvertently, be exposing them to the growing number of distractions and the forces of darkness currently raging in the world. It is to avoid such situations as well as help grandparents and parents to have the resource materials to teach their children and grandchildren at home that the three different volumes of this book have been produced. This, hopefully, will fill a part of the growing gap that many of the distractions, including the ravaging coronavirus pandemic, have caused in the world.

As we are now in a new era of 'distant learning' and the observance of social distance in interpersonal communication, many schools and institutions of higher learning will no longer function in the way they were originally intended, to teach pupils and lecture students in close contact with face-to-face interaction. The 'new normal' has further separated pupils from their teachers and students from their lecturers.

Apart from this, the ever-changing government policies on education and the diminishing relationship between governments and parents in the school sector, have unarguably placed more responsibility on parents and grandparents in regard to the provision of adequate education for their loved ones. Grandparents, who are more home-based, more qualified and more experienced, especially in the area of passing on their faith to their children and grandchildren, now have a very unique responsibility to step in quickly to answer God's call in the area of faith transmission to the younger generation. This is the bell that has been ringing in the horizon since the pandemic broke out, and many seem not to have heard the sound. For this reason I am directing everyone's attention to this matter in this chapter and in the one immediately following.

Promoting Family Values and Spirituality

This has become necessary as the governments and organisations in the society we live in today have not made adequate provision for children and youths to receive long lasting moral and religious education, which would ultimately promote family values and family spirituality in the world.

Having known this, parents, especially the grandparents, must be ready to 'take the bull by the horn', as no one can actually act successfully on their behalf in transmitting their own knowledge and experience to their children and grandchildren. It is for this purpose – to encourage parents and grandparents to play active roles in the spiritual development of their children, grandchildren and their wards in the domestic church, that this chapter and the one following it are specifically designed to highlight how they can bring about spiritual revolutions in their families. The two chapters are also focused on the signs in the horizon and how these could be successfully employed to create spiritual revolutions that will make our world a better place for generations yet unborn to live in. To this end, it is crucial to identify, first and foremost, the roles that the parents and grandparents should play at different levels to salvage a situation where children and grandchildren in the home are currently finding it more and more uninteresting to devote quality time to prayers. Grandparents even find it more difficult these days to get their grandchildren to give some time to the reading and sharing of the Word of God from the scriptures during family devotion.

What has compounded this situation is the growing craze in the world for using computers to control every aspect of our individual lives. The ugliest and most condemnable situation we also find is that grandparents, children and grandchildren can be in the same house for two hours or more without talking to each other because everyone is busy on electronic devices playing video games, texting messages to friends or chatting with former or present classmates. This is quite shocking and disappointing as it has brought about less communication and less opportunity to receive clarification in respect to knotty issues in the home.

Passing On the Christian Faith to Grandchildren

It is an indisputable fact that when we read the bible every day, we learn a lot because it is wisdom coming from above, giving us clear indication on how to meander through life and stay at peace with our God and neighbour as we obey God's commandments and do his holy will. From history, we also learn that many generations before us learnt quite a lot from the same bible to gain wisdom, which propelled them to make the necessary sacrifices to be on the 'narrow path' to heaven. However, many who did not even read the bible learnt much about the sanctity of life and family values from their parents and grandparents.

Much of the learning was carried out through practical experiences of staying close to and working with their parents and grandparents as well as with elders in the community. Some of those personal experiences, which some of them took pains to document in books, have undeniably become great treasures that should not be disposed of quickly by our present and coming generations. For us to ensure that our grandchildren, children and youths do not lose the opportunity of hearing, learning and putting into practice the positive experiences of our older generations, it seems quite urgent for us, with the lockdowns we are experiencing in the world, to get grandparents to begin a new relationship with their own children and grandchildren for the purpose of the spiritual development of everyone in the domestic church. This will be the beginning point where many sacrifices should be urgently directed by grandparents if a significant impact is to be made in the transmission of the Christian faith to our children and grandchildren.

The first task before the grandparents in ensuring that there is a continuous transmission of faith to their children and grandchildren, in and out of season, is to have a thriving domestic church where the entire family collectively worship the living God. This is very important because what is practised at home will be imbibed easily by the children and grandchildren. They will most likely want to do the same themselves in the near future. The way to set up a thriving domestic church and how to sustain it has been sufficiently addressed in Volume One of this book, therefore it is unnecessary to dwell on this in this Volume Three.

Suffice it to state here that if children in a family are married and living separately from their parents, they also need to make their own domestic church functional and productive as they give their lives to Christ. In such a situation, grandparents will be happy to see if their own children have replicated what they learnt from them in their new homes. To ensure that things work well to the glory of God, grandparents must take on the added responsibility of visiting their children frequently to help them set up a thriving domestic church.

This is certainly a better gift to give to one's children than buying several cows to mark their wedding anniversary or buying them a car when a new baby is born into the family as one's grandchild. If the focus of grandparents is always on heavenly things, their children and grandchildren will know what to expect from their parents and grandparents. And they themselves will ultimately be focused on heavenly things instead of the material things that people will leave behind in this world.

The starting point to get one's children and grandchildren focused on heavenly things is to teach them the Ten Commandments of God, ensuring that they learn them by heart as well as the implications and the consequences of ignoring and/or deliberately disobeying any of them. To enable them to engrave these commandments in their hearts, they are reproduced here as clearly indicated in Deuteronomy 5:7–21:

> (1) You shall have no other gods before me. You shall not make for yourself a graven image, or any likeness of anything that is in heaven above, or that is in the earth beneath or that is in the water under the earth; you shall not bow down to them or serve them; for I the Lord your God am a jealous God, visiting the iniquity of the fathers upon the children to the third and

fourth generation of those who hate me, but showing merciful love to thousands of those who love me and keep my commandments.

(2) You shall not take the name of the Lord your God in vain: for the Lord will not hold him guiltless who takes his name in vain.

(3) Observe the sabbath day, to keep it holy as the Lord your God commanded you. Six days you shall labour, and do all your work; but the seventh day is a sabbath to the Lord your God; in it you shall not do any work, you, or your son, or your daughter, or your manservant, or your maidservant, or your ox, or your donkey, or any of your cattle, or the sojourner who is within your gates, that your manservant and maidservant may rest as well as you. You shall remember that you were a servant in the land of Egypt, and the Lord your God brought you out from where with a mighty hand and outstretched arm; therefore the Lord your God commanded you to keep the sabbath day holy.

(4) Honour your father and your mother, as the Lord your God commanded you; that your days may be prolonged, and that it may go well with you in the land which the Lord your God gives you.

(5) You shall not kill.

(6) You shall not commit adultery.

(7) You shall not steal.

(8) You shall not bear false witness against your neighbour.

(9) You shall not covet your neighbour's wife;

(10) And you shall not desire your neighbour's house, his field, or his manservant, or his maid servant, his ox, or his donkey, or anything that is your neighbour's.

This should be everybody's guiding compass. The grandparents are to help their children and grandchildren to memorise, understand and do all that is humanly possible not to disobey the commandments of God.

It is very important that as grandparents and parents regularly direct the attention of everyone in the household to God's commandments, they should also be disabusing their minds about being glued to their computer and television at the expense of losing their faith in God. The reason is that a majority of children learn all sorts of things from the internet, Facebook, Twitter, WhatsApp and all social media as well as from the electronic media that make a good number of them believe that obeying the Ten Commandments was only meant for the people of old, and not for the present generation.

This is coming from the fact that the evil messages beamed at them from social media and the other communication gadgets they parade around have changed their orientation, as they are being discouraged from moving towards the living God. So, any activity or duty that elders in the home assign to the children and grandchildren that is not computer-based is seen by them as quite boring, uninteresting and unsatisfying to undertake. Is there any wonder that it has become an uphill task to get children and youths to sit down for an hour or two to listen to the Word of God and participate in activities that will make them understand that we all need to build our treasure in heaven, and not on this earth as we sojourn on in life.

For different reasons culminating in self-interest, one sees that children and youths now prefer to deploy their energies and time to using computers mainly for entertaining themselves, solving their socio-economic problems and/or using it for ulterior motives. Suffice it to state that they have now perfected how to undertake many transactions through the internet, phone and the use of their credit or debit cards to have supplies delivered to them whether there is money in their bank account or not. Some have even learnt how to use these devices to steal money from people's bank accounts, carry out robberies and kidnap people in order to be paid a ransom before victims are released, etc. To them, life is simple and sweet, and so one can get rich quickly without much ado.

The negative thoughts and the evils associated with children and youths in society have become things of great concern for the Church. This explains why she has been rolling out different spiritual programmes to help to bring the minds of the derailed children and youths back to God. One of the successful programmes being organised by the Vatican to change the current orientation of many children and youths is the World Youth Day. This has been organised in different continents of the world already, but a lot of work still needs done at national, state, local, ward, zone and family levels. Organisations in the Church such as the Holy Family Society have no other choice than to key into the new evangelisation mission of the Church to stem the current trend of children and youths being deceived and/or discouraged by what they see or hear from social media, the internet, television, radio, etc., from obeying God's commandments.

The time has come when Church organisations such as the Holy Family Society should use the new evangelisation scheme of the Church to get Christian grandparents, just as the Apostles did in their time, to testify before those who are being misled today that it was not a mistake that God sent his beloved Son to this world to rescue the 'perverse generation' that abandoned God at a certain point in the world's history.

They are to remind everyone that when people of older generations were no longer observing the Ten Commandments, with many of them abandoning God completely, the Apostles had to speak point blank to the perverse generation that had gone other ways. They spoke with confidence to them, reminding everyone that, 'we did not follow cleverly devised myths when we made known to you the power and coming of our Lord Jesus Christ, but we were eyewitnesses of his majesty. For when he received honour and glory from God the Father and the voice was borne to him by the majestic glory, "This is my beloved Son, with whom I am well pleased", we heard the voice from heaven, for we were with him on the holy mountain' (2 Pt 1:16–18).

It is this type of witness that grandparents especially are being called upon to arm themselves with as they go out into the field to play their own role in the new evangelisation mission. Convinced that God has spoken to us all through his words recorded in the scriptures, and as he still speaks to us through many sources every day, we should all, no matter our position in life, be bold enough to go out to profess him and make him known to others.

Our evangelisation efforts should begin from our homes, hence the roles of the grandparents become relevant in the passing on of the faith. Pope Francis has bolstered our efforts by encouraging grandparents to come to the rescue. He has been hammering this point at every opportunity that he has had to speak to the elders of the Church. While speaking on the occasion of the Fifty-fourth World Communications Day on 24 May 2020, he also advised all involved in the new evangelisation mission to arm themselves with true life stories of themselves that can be seen as an 'appendix' to the bible.

In Volume One of this book, I had clarified that the Pope's advice about writing our own true-life stories is not for us to blow our own trumpets, but to present our faith in Jesus so that other people can also learn from this, apart from what they read in the bible. It is therefore in the interest of those who are lining up with the members of the Holy Family Society in the new evangelisation mission, especially grandparents, that a new evangelical force is mobilised to go out into the field to win souls for Christ. New messages directed to the inner hearts of the young ones in the community need to be quickly formulated. The way to go about this will become clearer as the reader progresses, reading from one chapter to the next, especially when it comes to learning about how to use the spiritual tools we have in the Church to grow in our own holiness and prepare for a holy death, which can happen at any time.

2
_____

The 'New Normal' and the Challenges for Parents and Grandparents

As indicated earlier in Chapter One of this volume on the domestic church, the place where a number of religious exercises should begin, exercises that are channelled towards the development of faith, is in the Christian home. This is now even more so as the coronavirus pandemic has imposed new challenges, which people also refer to as the 'new normal', on the whole world, requiring people to wear masks, stay six feet from each other and then stay at home rather than go out to do business or for schooling.

Parents and grandparents now need to play crucial roles in the organisation of new religious exercises to keep the faith of members of their household in order to face the challenges posed by the 'new normal'. This now calls for a new approach in making the domestic church more functional and all-involving as parents and grandparents could design spiritual programmes that will help develop the faith of everyone as people get involved in the following areas:

(1) Praying for Children and Grandchildren
This is a daily task that both grandparents and parents should take on board as their primary duty. Prayers of grandparents and parents can be described as sharper than a blade in the way they work and should therefore be directed towards positive ends. Prayers are to be freely

and joyfully poured on their children and grandchildren possibly on a daily basis to enable them to use the sharp ends of these tools as part of their spiritual security, while their guardian angels are also there to protect them. But the rights of the grown-up children and grandchildren to always have such sharp tools to defend themselves must be earned by each of them by not deliberately and/or stubbornly doing things that are neither pleasing to their parents and grandparents nor to their own guardian angels. Once a child avoids this, his or her parents or grandparents cannot have any justification for denying this child their blessings. It is therefore very important for parents to pray for their children and grandchildren.

It must be noted here that parents' and grandparents' blessings, which come from their inner hearts, are sanctioned by God, hence many children and grandchildren who receive such blessings prosper in life. There is no doubting the fact that those who think that the blessings from parents and grandparents do not matter, and therefore turn against them to incur their curses, encounter a lot of hardship in life. They end up without really reaping the fruits of their labour. I myself have witnessed a few examples of this but it is unwise and unnecessary to mention families where such happenings can be verified. The important thing here is to give good training to children and grandchildren from the beginning so that when they grow older they do not constitute nuisance to society and/or take up arms against their parents and grandparents.

To avoid such situations, or seeing children and youths joining immoral, dangerous gangs, efforts must be made from the beginning to give them good moral and religious training from the home. During such training, one of the fundamental truths the children and grandchildren must be told is that they are not allowed to be so offended as to shower insults on their parents and grandparents. In various cultures of the world, this is not permissible because there could be serious consequences for the children who utter such insults. Therefore, children and grandchildren are to be told from an early age that whatever wrongs they believe have been done to them by their parents or grandparents, they should never take up arms against them or go to the extent of showering abuses on them. Instead, they should always go back to their parents and grandparents, like the prodigal son, to mend fences with them. The blessings they will receive from their parents and/or grandparents for doing this will follow them throughout their lifetime. Such an act from children or grandchildren shows their agape love, patience, forgiveness and humility.

Once children and grandchildren begin to cultivate these virtues from the beginning, they will become part and parcel with them. And if they grow up still putting these virtues into practice, certainly nothing will prevent them from being prosperous. They will also have long life as promised by our Creator. A child who honours his or her parents has long life awaiting him or her as clearly indicated in the fourth commandment, which says: 'Honour your father or your mother, as the Lord your God commanded you; that your days may be prolonged, and that it may go well with you, in the land which the Lord your God has given you' (Deut 5:16).

It is therefore of great importance that parents and grandparents put into practice the virtue of forgiveness as well as cultivate the habit of saying prayers every day for their children and grandchildren, as these can turn them around even if they are not meeting certain expectations. It is needless to emphasise here that no one in the family, including the children and grandchildren, should ignore prayer as it works wonders. This explains why parents and grandparents should place prayer as an item of top priority to make their domestic church function effectively for the benefit of all in the household.

(2) Preparing Guidelines for Children and Grandchildren

Before the children and grandchildren grow up to adulthood, their parents and grandparents have the responsibility to introduce to them a set of life guidelines or golden rules from the beginning that are expected to be observed by everyone in the household. Such guidelines are to help the children and grandchildren to learn good habits, which they can cultivate and make part and parcel of them throughout their lives. Once this is done from the beginning, these rules become part and parcel of everyone in the household. This is the way to have an orderly home.

From the guidelines set by the grandparents or parents as the case may be, everyone in the household should know when to wake up every morning and be ready for prayer; when to do physical exercise, when to get ready for morning Mass, when to get ready for school or work, when to be at the breakfast table, when to leave for school or work and when to return, when to do school assignments and carry out house chores, when to relax, watch films, play computer games or take a nap, when everyone should be at the dinner table and when to say night prayers before going to bed, etc.

If grandparents or parents prepare time schedules for these and make great efforts to implement them, there will undoubtedly be orderliness in the home, and the children and grandchildren who comply with the rules will not be lacking in many respects in the future. This is the essence of getting everyone in the house to key into a good pattern of orderly life from the home. And when the children and grandchildren grow up and set out on their own, they will not set the guidelines aside because they will have seen the benefits they derived from implementing them during their growing years.

What is conventionally known as the golden rule is stated clearly in Matthew 7:12, for everyone in the household to also adopt. It is clearly stated therein that: 'So whatever you wish that men would do to you, do so to them, for this is the law and the prophets'. If everyone in one's family adopts this and uses it as a guiding compass, there will be less evil in our society.

(3) Educating Children and Grandchildren on the Sanctity of Human Life

Grandparents also have the unique responsibility of educating their children and grandchildren about the sanctity of the human life. This should be emphasised in the domestic church from time to time, especially during the reflections on the scripture passages relating to God's injunction: 'Be fruitful, multiply and fill the earth' (Gn 9:1). From the reflections on this gospel message, members of one's household will realise that God's valid instruction to us is to be fruitful and co-create human beings with him, to eventually fill the earth. He did not give anyone the license to terminate the life of any other person at any stage. If this message is brought home to the understanding of the children and grandchildren right from their formative years, they will not contemplate the idea of committing or sponsoring abortion in any form in the future.

(4) Teaching Family Values to Children and Grandchildren

This is where our traditional teachings on family values come into play. In our African tradition, children and grandchildren are taught from an early age how to greet elders in the morning at first sight, without which it becomes an offense, even if the person who missed the first opportunity decided to do it three times more. This is followed by another lesson on how to respect one's elders, especially parents and grandparents. For instance, if a young child sees their father or mother come into a sitting room in which they were watching a television programme, they should immediately get up to welcome him or her and be ready to answer their questions. The volume of television is to be immediately lowered or completely turned off. This is to show respect for them and to be able to listen to them as they pass on instructions. But most often these days, children neither pay attention to the presence of their parents nor have time to look elsewhere other than at whatever they are watching on the television or the computer game they are playing from their handset.

To engage the children in a manner that their hearts and minds are not hijacked by the menacing computer games, which are many a time accompanied by evil stories/cartoons and corrupting messages, parents and grandparents are to see that they allocate time for their children to do their homework, as well as set out times in their schedule for them to do their house chores. They must, in addition, be taught the following: how to cook, how to sweep, how to clean bathrooms, how to dress their beds, how to stand for elders to sit, especially in a place where chairs are not sufficiently provided, how to assist the elderly to wash and iron their clothes, how to share whatever food that is available with one another, how to persevere in the face of difficulties, how to assist the poor and the vulnerable in the community, etc.

And to uphold long cherished family values, children and youths must be made to understand that it is a taboo for siblings and other members of the extended family to be involved in sexual intercourse and that cousins up to the fourth generations cannot be accepted to have marriages conducted between them. If these and many more are taught to the children in the comfort of their homes, they will forever cherish their upbringing and the family values that their parents, grandparents and the community hold so dear. What should be clear to all and sundry, especially grandparents, is: 'Train up a child in the way he should go, and when he is old, he will not depart from it' (Prov 22:6).

(5) Teaching on Integrity

When observing what is happening around the world, we find that people seem more comfortable these days to tell lies even at the highest office in the land to enable them to swing people to their own side of the story or to gain political points. Such situations have brought a lack of integrity to the socio-political and economic landscape throughout the world. This has also brought a lack of trust to certain men of God who preach the Word of God from the two sides of their mouths. It is unfortunate that many political leaders, government functionaries, business owners and Chief Executives as well as many religious preachers in the world today 'turn away from listening to the truth and wander into myths' (2 Tm 4:4), thereby creating calamities, commotions and uncertainties in the universe.

It is to avoid this, that grandparents and others must use the domestic church to teach children and grandchildren the essence of maintaining high integrity by telling the truth all the time. It is very important to remind ourselves here that Jesus encouraged us to always be prepared to tell the truth at all times, especially if we are desirous of being members of his flock.

We should not mind the circumstances we are faced with, we should be ready to let the truth come from us. Jesus told the Jews in John 8:32, and by extension his message is for all of us, that: 'the truth will make you free'. And that 'when the spirit of truth comes, he will guide you into all the truth for he will not speak on his own authority, but whatever he hears he will speak, and he will declare to you the things that are to come' (Jn 16:13). From this message we are also to note that by telling the truth, we help ourselves to build up a positive image in society.

(6) Paying Great Importance to Visits and Welcoming Strangers
It is important that parents and grandparents teach in the domestic church the importance of going with members of the household to visit elders in the extended family. This promotes unity in the extended family system, which is highly cherished in Africa. There is also the dire need to take members of one's family to pay frequent visits to other places like the hospitals, orphanages, rehabilitation homes and prison yards. The visits to such places bring the message of Christ presented in Matthew 25:31–46 home, to be well rooted in the hearts of everyone, including the children and youths in the home.

Through practical examples of welcoming strangers into the home, many children and grandchildren will also get to understand the biblical injunction that we should be our brother's keeper. This gesture of visiting people and welcoming strangers should be developed to become a tradition in the family, having known that great reward awaits those who put this into practice. It should be made known to all that on Judgement Day one can have the reward of being accepted into heaven because of our having made it a habit to visit and care for those in dire need.

The gospel message in Matthew 25:31–46 should be read regularly to the hearing of everyone, so that all will understand what awaits each and every one of us if we are generous with our time, and if we freely welcome strangers into our homes.

(7) Going on Spiritual Pilgrimages to Holy Places and Shrines

As grandparents groom their loved ones in the domestic church, it is important that members of the household are sometimes taken along on spiritual pilgrimages to holy places and shrines. This will expose everyone to a deeper knowledge of what is written in the bible. If such a journey of faith is undertaken, the significant difference it could make in the lives of the people cannot be easily quantified. As expected, the tour guide tries quite often to bring the scriptural stories to everyone's understanding to enable all to feel as if the events from over two thousand years ago have only recently taken place.

Going on spiritual pilgrimages is very important in building up our faith. The spiritual pilgrimages can also, because of lack of adequate funding, be undertaken in our communities or within our country, provided that good religious sites are chosen. The important thing is to find a lonely place that one can take members of one's family to, like the way Jesus found lonely places to pray, sometimes by himself and sometimes with his Apostles.

In such open, lonely places, one is able to appreciate nature as well as God's infinite love and mercy, and then use the period to evaluate one's life in order to recognise previous wrongdoings, with a view to making immediate amendments. This helps a lot to reconcile oneself with God and with those whom one has offended in the course of one's daily work and interaction with people. And once those who undertake such a family pilgrimage follow this up by going to confession, they will definitely notice a significant improvement in their spiritual lives. So, parents and grandparents have significant roles to play in encouraging members of their household to undertake family spiritual pilgrimages from time to time.

(8) Teaching on Sacrifices and Selflessness

In today's world where people, including parents, children and youths are thinking more on what they need to acquire from day to day in order to live a successful life, it becomes apparent that grandparents must intervene quickly to redirect their interest to something more meaningful and heavenly rewarding. That is, making sacrifices for the benefits of others and working selflessly for the sake of the kingdom. These are twin seeds that must be planted in the domestic church so that all members of the household will jointly nurture them to see that they grow successfully in everyone. If these twin seeds grow into a big tree with branches that form comfortable shade that can cover everyone in the household, many will be energised to plant similar twin seeds when they move out to begin their own family life elsewhere.

The lessons on sacrifices and selflessness were well demonstrated by our Lord Jesus Christ himself who spent forty days and forty nights in the desert, without a place to sleep, nor well prepared food to eat, all in a great effort to prepare himself as God-man to face the intrigues, torture and wickedness of men in the world. As God-man, he was already aware of the type of problems he was going to confront in the world when his mission began. So, he had to spend such a number of days and nights in the lonely desert to prepare himself spiritually to undertake his mission of coming into the world to show to everyone that he is 'the Way, the Truth and the Life' (Jn 14:6). He also solidly prepared to announce to the world that: 'he who hears the word and understands it; he indeed bears fruit, and yields, in one case a hundredfold, in another sixty, and in another thirty' (Mt 13:23). Jesus further clarified that those who do his Father's will here on earth will win eternal life, pointing out that he is the light of the world and those who follow him will 'not walk in darkness but will have the light of life' (Jn 8:12). And to demonstrate what selflessness and making sacred sacrifice means, he gave himself up when he could have beckoned on the angels of God to save him. Instead, he called on God, saying: 'My Father, if it is possible, let this chalice pass from me, nevertheless, not as I will, but as you will' (Mt 26:39).

To further demonstrate the length one can go to in making sacrifices for the friends one loves so much, Jesus paid the supreme sacrifice with his life by submitting himself to be nailed on the cross, and dying a shameful death. Before this, Jesus himself had testified that, 'Greater love has no man that a man lay down his life for his friends. You are my friends ... I have called you friends, for all I have heard from my Father I have made known to you' (Jn 15:13–15).

Jesus has shown us how to make great sacrifices for one another, grandparents have to teach this in the domestic church by demonstrating in the simplest form how children and grandchildren can make sacrifices for one another and for people that are considered to be less privileged in society. If family members from different homes learn this, it will have a great impact in general on our society, as we would observe people making valuable and lasting sacrifices for their family, friends, community, state, nation and the world at large.

(9) Participating in the Activities and Projects of the Church and Community

It is a good thing for parents and grandparents to also introduce to their children and grandchildren what it takes to be active participants in the programmes and projects of the Church and of the community in which one lives. Members of the household should be taught that participating in any activity or project requires one to be involved in all or any of the following: praying for the success of the project, deploying time to be physically present from time to time to cheer up and bring some comfort to those at the place of the project's execution, as well as other aspects relating to the execution such as the free deployment of one's energy and talents, donating funds, hiring people for part-execution, soliciting for funds, helping to process certain documentations for the execution, providing food and drinks for those at the site of execution, providing transportation to and from the site, providing security men at the site, etc.

With grandparents emphasising these matters in the domestic church as crucial areas where people can be involved in Church or community projects, it will help members of the household to always find a space where they themselves can identify with a good intentioned, communal project. If this is discussed frequently with parents and grandparents showing good examples on how to be engaged in such projects, the children and grandchildren will be learning something that will be completely outside of the subjects they are taught in schools.

In so doing, the children and youths will naturally feel obliged to be part and parcel of those involved in Church and community projects being executed in their area. This is the way the young ones in a household can grow to become good donors and further grow in such acts to become dependable philanthropists. It is needless to emphasise here that good donors never lack, and they certainly have a heavenly reward awaiting them as they genuinely help to promote God's kingdom here on earth.

(10) Teaching People How to Be Close to the Church and to God
Apart from encouraging the members of one's household to be good donors to Church or community projects, the grandparents cannot but also make it clear to the young family members that there are still other ways to be close to the Church and to God. All of these, however, also border on rendering selfless services with one's energy, time, talent, treasures and/or life. Such works that are of great importance to the Church and to the community include: sweeping the Church and the streets, cleaning the Church's pews, teaching Sunday school children, teaching catechism classes for different

categories of people preparing for baptism and confirmation, teaching marriage classes for those preparing for marriage, serving at Mass in the Church, singing during Mass as a member of the choir, serving as a Church warden to ensure orderliness during Mass, deciding to give one's entire life to God by going to the seminary to study for priesthood, or in the case of others going into religious life, supporting the Church by sponsoring anyone in the seminary or religious life, providing welfare and medical needs to priests and religious, participating in the building of a town hall, giving scholarships to students in the community, providing sporting equipment to schools, etc.

Since rendering these types of selfless services can bring one closer to the Church, to the community and to God, parents and grandparents are to show good examples to their loved ones on how to make great sacrifices towards this objective. The best place for grandparents to speak on the services enumerated above is in the domestic church. This will help to enlighten children and grandchildren in their growing years on the types of services they themselves can render freely to the Church.

If children and grandchildren in the home continue to entertain such thoughts and follow them up with positive actions as they grow older, they will find themselves working in the vineyard and moving closer and closer to God, who created each and every one of us. It is only when this seed of nurturing children and grandchildren is well planted by grandparents and continuously watered by parents that the seed will grow into a large tree. The direct result of this is that the tree will continuously produce good fruits that will help to sustain as well as bring good improvements to the Church and to the community. This explains why grandparents have a greater responsibility to participate in the building, equipping and sustaining of the Church as well as the domestic church.

(11) Teaching on Sex Before Marriage and Sex Outside of Marriage

The lack of knowledge on this topic of youths preparing for marriage and of many who are already married has pushed many in the community into immoral acts. In the past, people have depended on the Church to educate them on the question of whether or not engaged couples or couples planning to be engaged can cohabit and have sexual intercourse before their marriage. Many do not even know anything about this, until sometimes even three months before their wedding when some of them must have been cohabiting for one or two years. It is only then that they will realise that they have been committing grievous sin.

For some of them, it is only after they have registered for a three-month pre-marital course that they come to the understanding that they were not supposed to have been cohabiting or engaging themselves in sexual acts before marriage. Although some of them may have received some information about this when they were preparing for their first Holy Communion during their growing years, they may well have forgotten this in their adulthood.

So, the domestic church where grandparents can use their wisdom and maturity to explain the consequences of immoral acts before marriage and outside of marriage should now be profitably employed to deal with this matter. Children and grandchildren who are of age and looking forward to marital life should not simply be waiting for the three-month marriage course before seeking useful information from their parents, grandparents, or their would-be sponsors to enable them to understand what they need to take along into marital life. If the information is lacking from home, the intending couple will have missed a lot as the three-month marriage course being organised in parishes cannot be said to be adequate.

For the Church to address this issue, it would mean that her curriculum would need to be reviewed and extended to cover very relevant topics on marital life such as pregnancy within and outside of marriage, sanctity in marriage, sexual abuse of one's own children, denial of sexual intercourse in marriage, how to settle minor and/or serious quarrels, abstinence from sex, owning property, work challenges, care for the children, sex outside marriage, etc. Some of these subjects are many a time missing in the organised three-month marriage course in the parish. Because of the lack of knowledge in some crucial aspects of marital life, there has been a lot of promiscuity and immorality in very many marriages, leading to the breakup of many homes.

A typical example can be given here. On Saturday, 8 August 2020, Rev. Fr John Paul Ojuikpai, in his humility and good sense of duty, posted this message in the National WhatsApp platform of the Holy Family Society in order to seek urgent assistance in solving a delicate marriage problem:

A Married Man Had Three Children Outside His Marriage Before Reconciling With His First Wife. How Do I Help Him?

Please, how do l help this man? He had a problem with his wife with whom he wedded and had four children before they separated. After about five years, the man married another woman with whom he didn't wed at all and the woman had about three children with him but she is not coming to the Catholic Church. The first wife returned and reconciled with this same man. The man is asking what will he do now? Will the mother Church allow him and the formal wife to live together again?

Please help me oh, I'm just two years as a priest in a remote village. Cure me of coming Tuesday office fever.

Rev. Fr John Paul Ojuikpai
Parish Priest,
St Martin's Catholic Church, Oso Edda, Abakaliki Diocese

Immediately, on the same day, he received the following responses:

First Response:
Good evening and happy weekend. In the actual sense, before the Church, the wife that is legitimately wedded in Church is your wife. Without impediment, no divorce is ever possible and excepting in cases of unpardonable impurities with regard to the sixth commandment or of uncultured temper that could lead to death or threaten meaningful life, no separation is necessary. Thus, even if they had lived apart, they remain married before God and man. And the third party is truly an intruder.

However, now that children are involved, care must be taken not to throw the innocent into anguish. Thus, while he reconciles with his first wife, he should talk peaceably with the other woman. Then, let them go and see their Parish Priest. Thanks.

Rev. Fr Osemhantie Okhueleigbe
Personal Secretary to Archbishop Patrick Ekpu
(Archbishop Emeritus of Benin City)

Second Response:
Good evening Fr JP. Thanks for sharing this. The Church's position is very clear on this. Even if the first wife never returned, but still breathes, *without an annulment* of the marriage, she remains the recognised wife of the man (irrespective of the fact that he is now married to another woman). Moreover, no Catholic minister would have even witnessed his second marriage – meaning the second marriage is a case of adultery, not marriage. For the fact that the first wife returned, it's very clear that their union was never annulled, hence, she remains the recognised wife.

In this case, the Church's position is that the man must henceforth no longer have a 'husband and wife' relationship with the supposedly second woman (not wife), yet must continue his fatherly responsibilities to the woman's children (while relating with their mother like a brother, not a husband).

Rev. Fr Henry Nkemakolam Emeka
Assistant Parish Priest of Christ the King Catholic Church, Magwi County
Eastern Equitoria State, South Sudan

Having seen what has been proffered as solutions to the complex marital problem from fellow priests, this author quickly contributed the piece below:

Third Response:
Good Arrangements but Much More to Do!
Father Henry, thanks a lot for your candid advice and for making known the Church's position on the issue. Let me also thank Father John Paul for his efforts to solve the man-made problem.

Since the couple are now together with a joint resolve to continue with their marriage, one needs to congratulate them first and foremost for this bold decision. With this decision, it is clear that a major part of the problem has been resolved. It seems clear also to the couple that the Church will not have granted them annulment, if nothing really invalidated the marriage on day it was celebrated.

So, their decision to come together is sixty per cent of the problems solved. Efforts must be made to solve the remaining problems.

To this end, it will not be out of place to encourage the legitimately married couple to make time to renew their commitment to each other possibly in a private chapel in the presence of their priest, children, friends and well-wishers. Before this, they could also seek the help of a psychologist to prepare their hearts and minds for spiritual uplifting and building of trust for one another.

Both of them would need to pledge not to entertain ill-thoughts against the other woman who will now be like a 'sister' not only to the man but also to his legitimate wife. The children already begotten by the 'sister' must be accepted and cared for in the same way the children from the legitimate wife are cared for. This is usually a difficult task for the legitimate wife to handle. This is why counselling is seriously needed, for all the parties, including the 'sister' and her children.

Until their 'sister' is married to another man, the man has a responsibility to continue to provide for her in terms of paying her house rent and giving her feeding allowance. The only thing the man cannot do again with the 'sister' is to have sexual relationship with her. It is to avoid this that the man should immediately rent a separate apartment for the 'sister' to live in as soon as the legitimate wife returned fully to his house.

It is also because of the unhealthy situation which infidelity and procreation outside marriage usually cause that married men are often told not to use their own hands to create multifaceted problems for themselves, and for their God-given families.

Apart from the resultant new financial commitments the man has to face, he has also unavoidably placed himself under the watchful eyes not only of his legitimate wife, but also of the children, the parishioners and 'tale-bearers' that have since engaged themselves to be giving daily reports.

From now on, any story, whether true or false, about the man's continuous dealings with the 'sister' is bound to blow him up to a state of anguish and trauma. This is why the man has to tread with caution and seek the help of a psychologist from time to time.

It will therefore be helpful if Fr John Paul will invite all parties, one after the other, to let them know the implications of the possible arrangements that have to take place because of the new development. When he discovers that the arrangements are virtually accepted by all sides after speaking to them separately, then he can ask them to come together on a fixed date, with each side bringing a witness. And if all the parties agree to such joint meeting to resolve the issues, then Father can invite two elders of the Church to be with him to resolve the issues. The Father could ask the parties if they will want a video recording of the meeting, along with having also the resolutions signed by all the parties.

If the answer is negative but agrees to resolve their problems in the presence of the Blessed Sacrament, Fr John Paul should take them for their words and go ahead to conclude the arrangements. At the next opportunity, the Father should congratulate them in the presence of the whole congregation for happily resolving their marital problems and ask the congregation to continue to pray for the sustenance of their marriage. This, to my mind, will be a way to resolve the issue, which may not be completely satisfactory to all parties. There is no doubting it that each party, including the children in the marriage, will lose something in the whole arrangement. It is our prayer that the Almighty God will usher in a new era of peace, love and unity for the married couple while their 'sister' will also find her new home soonest.

Sir David E. Osunde
Founder, Holy Family Society

While the advice contained in the three responses above cannot be said to be perfect, it clearly indicates how complex infidelity, having children outside marriage, separation in marriage, etc., can be. The underlying message is that it is better for married couples not to use their own hands to create complex problems that will live with them and their children forever in their homes.

(12) Grandparents for Urgent Rescue Mission

Having seen that the coronavirus pandemic has foisted a 'new normal' upon the world, restricting movements and making people stay more at home, it has become quite urgent for the grandparents to organise themselves into a formidable group that will regularly exchange their ideas and experiences in life, as well as how to deal with the multiplying number of problems of youths in the community. To this end, the Holy Family Society intends to launch a new sub-project shortly, titled: 'Elders and Youths Connection'. This will be under the auspices of the Grandparents Council that is also already in the front burner of the society. In order to get everyone involved, the society wants those below fifty years of age to consider themselves as youths while those above fifty years should see themselves as elders.

The idea is to have a veritable forum where elders will engage the youths in constant dialogue with a view to transmitting their Christian faith and our long-cherished family values to them. This new project involves bringing grandparents, children and youths together with their young parents to engage themselves in constant dialogue on issues about life, the family institutions, and worthy Christian practices. One cogent reason for this is that many parents of these days have not learnt enough themselves and so do not have much in these areas to pass on to their children, especially as they do not even show any interest in learning more about the good legacies they can leave behind for their children.

This author has personally observed with great appreciation and admiration the concern of our Holy Father, Pope Francis, for our children and youths all over the world, who seemed to be drifting away without parental guidance. Pope Francis therefore recommends that opportunities be created in our communities for the transmission of faith by grandparents to our youths to help them stay on the right paths of life where they will constantly encounter Christ, our Saviour.

Taking a further look into the Pope's appeal to grandparents, I find it quite urgent for the Holy Family Society to incorporate this project into its current family apostolate, with a view to bringing parents, grandparents and youths together for the proposed intensive interactions, knowing that our goal is to get fathers, mothers and their children walking on the right paths of life that will help them to win eternal life.

The Need for Everyone to Uphold the Christian Faith

As earlier indicated, there are many distractions in the world today that are making a good number of people lose their Christian faith. It is no news that the children and youths of today learn more from the smartphones, internet, social media and television than from their parents and grandparents. The direct consequence of this is that parents and grandparents have been finding it difficult to use their own knowledge of computers and the internet to direct their children and grandchildren appropriately on what to do to follow the path of life. This obviously involves upholding and teaching the Christian faith using smartphones and computers to get the young ones interested in the message one is to deliver to them.

For instance, to teach them the Ten Commandments, the young ones will prefer to be shown on the smartphone where they can read them, rather than showing them in the bible, which they find difficult to carry around, even to the Church.

Having seen the disposition of the young ones and how many of them are drifting away unknowingly from the Christian faith because of the negative influence of the internet, social media, and other electronic media that transmit very immoral messages, something drastic has to be done quickly to stem the tide.

The Church has also seen that many young parents of these days do not have the correct disposition towards religious issues and so do not have adequate scriptural knowledge to share and pass on to their children. Many of the young parents are unfortunately confused these days by many pastors who exhibit wealth all over the place and teach nothing but the 'gospel of prosperity'.

By following these so-called pastors, many young parents have unknowingly left their own children to be hoodwinked by what they find on the internet. We should see this as a great challenge to everyone to quickly create a forum for grandparents and elders in our midst to have regular interactive sessions with youths where they can pass on their knowledge and experiences to the present and coming generations.

Exposing Youths to Practical Experiences of Elders
The type of education to be imparted to the young ones through new schemes should be principally focused on, among other subjects, the knowledge and wisdom that one gains by daily reading of the bible, the sharing of practical experiences of the elders in the community, the problems youths encounter in our society, how to avoid immorality in order to stay in good health, how to promote good eating habits in order to stay healthy, physical exercises and the benefits from them, spiritual exercises that can help uplift the faith, how to use the internet profitably and how to prevent children from being led astray, the need to join solidarity movements and how to profit from them, promoting holiness and sainthood by showing and directing children and youths to historical texts on a number of saints on their smartphones, the need for family prayer and the unity it brings to the family, learning and putting into practice the virtues of Jesus, Mary and Joseph, speaking about the need to embrace priestly or religious life, etc. These are a few subject matters that can be added to others during formal meetings of elders and youths in the community.

It is important to emphasise here that the lectures on the different subjects are to be carefully designed to constantly provoke positive interactions at the regular sessions between elders and youths. This will go a long way in inculcating the Christian faith and our long-cherished family values in the participants. And if such lectures are transmitted online to many homes in the world, they will certainly make a great impact on all those who have the opportunity of viewing them online.

The Pope has given us a useful indication that for us to make a good start in this apostolate and for the children and youths to have a fulfilled life, all of them, no matter their age, must, first and foremost, recognise those who gave life to them by honouring them as stated in the fourth commandment. This is to make the children and youths receptive to what they are to learn from their parents and grandparents. Pope Francis admonished that 'achieving a full and happy life depends on proper recognition of those who brought us into the world'. He further advised that 'if you are distant from your parents, make an effort and return, go back to them; perhaps they are elderly ... They gave you life ... One should never insult a mother, never insult a father. Never, Never!'.[1]

Apart from respecting our own parents, Pope Francis urged all children to make a vow by saying from now, 'I will never insult anyone's mother or father. They gave life! They must never be insulted'.[2]

The Pope's message on honouring parents and grandparents was published on page three of *L'Osservatore Romano*, edition of Friday 21 September 2018. He sent out this message to prepare a good ground for inculcating Christian principles as well as the Church teachings from time immemorial in our children and youths. This can only be achieved when children and youths honour their parents, stay close to them for advice and support them in their old age.

Having covered a lot of ground on this matter already, it seems that what we also need to embark on in order to be successful in carrying out this aspect of our evangelisation mission, is to get the associations of grandparents in different parts of the world networking as they pursue a common goal for the benefit of our youths. These could either come under existing apostolate groups or

---

[1] Pope Francis, General Audience 19 September 2018, Vatican.
[2] Pope Francis, 19 September 2018, Vatican.

be designed to operate as new bodies. For instance, the Holy Family Society has in its front burner already the idea to formally inaugurate a Council of Grandparents to pursue similar objectives.

Such associations or councils should be able to network within the country and create good working relationships with similar bodies that have been set up outside our borders to pursue this same cause.

It was for this purpose that I used the opportunity of my attendance at the Ninth World Meeting of Families in Dublin, Ireland, in 2018, to seek collaborative efforts with the Catholic Grandparents Association already on the ground in many countries of the world. There, we also learnt the fact that Pope Benedict XVI (now emeritus) has also been quite passionate about setting up such associations in different parts of the world. To further lend his support to the work of the association, Pope Benedict XVI wholeheartedly composed a prayer in 2018, for grandparents, to help their cause of making domestic churches always produce good fruits in the world as they thrive successfully.

Below is the prayer composed by Pope Benedict XVI (emeritus) for grandparents:

Prayer for Grandparents
Lord Jesus, You were born of the Virgin Mary, the daughter of saints Joachim and Anne.

Look with love on grandparents the world over. Protect them! They are sources of enrichment for families, for the Church and for all of society. Support them! As they grow older, may they continue to be for their families strong pillars of Gospel faith, guardians of noble domestic ideals, living treasuries of sound religious traditions. Make them teachers of wisdom and courage that they may pass on to future generations the fruits of their mature human and spiritual experience.

Lord Jesus, help families and society to value the presence and the role of grandparents. May they never be ignored or excluded, but always encounter respect and love. Help them to live serenely and to feel welcomed in all the years of life which you give them. Mary, Mother of all the living, keep grandparents constantly in your care, accompany them on their earthly pilgrimage, and by your prayers, grant that all families may one day be reunited in our heavenly homeland, where you await all humanity for the great embrace of life without end. Amen!

With this prayer being said for grandparents all over the world, I am quite optimistic that those who genuinely embrace the new apostolate will make a great success of it. This is where we draw the curtain for this chapter.

3

The Sacrament of Confession: An Important Spiritual Tool to Make the Domestic Church Effective

The domestic church, like any magnificent, long-lasting structure, must be built on very solid pillars to make it run effectively. First and foremost, there must be quality leadership as well as the personal commitments of leaders of a home to live prayerful lives, as these are essential ingredients required for the setting up and sustenance of a domestic church. These aspects are as important as having high quality materials for the construction of a building that will eventually become a home for people to live in. Once leadership in the home is good and shows high level of commitment, worshipping God in spirit and in truth, one can then say there is a viable domestic church since God himself has assured that 'where two or three are gathered in my name, there am I in the midst of them' (Mt18:20).

However, it is still very important at this point to lay bare the qualities to expect from the leadership of a home to make the domestic church stand on a solid foundation.

Strong Catholic Faith Leads to the Setting up of a Thriving Domestic Church

After their wedding, the husband and wife, who exercise leadership in the family, are expected to begin their new journey demonstrating that they are now sacramentally married and this will be shown in the way they organise their family as a domestic church. This gives them a solid base on which to build their marital life and also helps them greatly to set up a thriving domestic church. As a sacramentally married couple, it is expected that they would have long been baptised and confirmed in the faith in accordance with the Catholic Church tradition, during which period they must have learnt much about the Catholic faith, as well as her 'dos' and 'don'ts'. It is because of their background knowledge of the Catholic faith that on the day of their wedding, they solemnly pledged to bring up their children in the love and fear of God. They pledge this because they themselves believe that 'the fear of the Lord leads to life; and he who has it rests satisfied; and he will not be visited by harm' (Prov 19:23).

So, for married couples to place their children in the right setting from the beginning, where they fear and love God all the days of their lives, it becomes their onerous duty to ensure that any child God blesses them with receives early baptism and confirmation in the Catholic Church.

When the married couples themselves have a good background in the Catholic faith, and further commit themselves to live a holy life, it will be easy for them to set up a functioning domestic church where their own children will play active roles.

A domestic church will not only be built on a solid ground but can be handled effectively by the father and mother who have given themselves completely to Christ and are desirous of worshipping God in spirit and in truth. The domestic church with this type of good leadership as indicated above is expected to function like a local, outstation Church without the celebration of the Holy Eucharist since the leaders there are not ordained. However, because lay persons play an effective role during the celebration of the Mass in a parish church, it is not out of place for lay persons in the home to play the same valuable part while they are in their family devotion.

What to Do Daily in a Domestic Church

Those participating in the family devotion are expected to know when all are to gather at the designated place in the morning and/or evening, depending on when it is most suitable for the majority. As members of the household gather together, they could begin with the rosary, requesting our Mother Mary to seek from her Son, our Lord Jesus Christ, pardon for their sins, and for all to have fruitful results in all their engagements on that day as well as have his protection from the hands of the evil one in society.

After the recitation of the holy rosary, the members of the family including the parents could submit their prayer intentions so that these can all be put together as the Prayers of the Faithful. The reading of these should come after the readings of the day and after two or three members of the family have shared the message they have received from these readings. A few minutes are then given for personal reflections before the Prayers of the Faithful are read. Thereafter, selected prayers from the Holy Family Society Book or other traditional prayers of the Church could be jointly recited by everyone to bring the family devotion to a close.

It should be noted here that before the recitation of the holy rosary and in between each decade, inspiring songs to honour our Mother Mary could be joyfully rendered. In addition, the praying household could also render some songs dedicated to the Holy Family of Nazareth before or after the Prayers of the Faithful, and then conclude the devotion with a closing anthem of the Holy Family Society, titled: 'And So Help Me God'. The household that jointly makes a commitment to go through this routine everyday will certainly experience peace and tranquility in the home as God himself will live happily with them.

Absence of the Celebration of the Holy Eucharist in a Domestic Church

It should be emphasised here that the absence of the celebration of the Holy Eucharist should not make the baptised persons in the home bother much about being in a state of grace before family devotion. What should be uppermost in the minds of the people is how to use any available opportunity they have to go for confession in their parish Church, Mass Centre, retreat centre, or at any other institutions where Catholic priests could be available on demand. The fact must be stressed that members of the household, particularly those who are baptised, should not forget their obligations to remain in a state of grace by making regular use of the sacrament of penance in order to be in good relationship with Christ, who works through the ordained Catholic priests to forgive us our sins.

All in the household, especially if they are Catholics must recognise the fact that our Lord Jesus Christ has given power to the ordained Catholic priests to hear our confessions and invoke his power to forgive all our sins as we confess them. He gave them power to do this when he told the Apostles, which through the ages has been passed to the ordained priest of God, 'whatever you bind on earth shall be bound in heaven, and whatever you loose on earth shall be loosed in heaven' (Mt 18:18).

If members of the household recognise this fact and often have their sins absolved through the sacrament of penance to improve their relationship with God, as well as open their home to welcoming strangers to worship God with them, they will consciously and assuredly be climbing the ladder of holiness in answer to the universal call to holiness.

Let it be re-emphasised here that because we are all sinners, we need to avail ourselves of the opportunity of going to confession at least once in a year during the Lenten period or before the end of the Easter period. The sacrament of penance is a great gift, which our Lord Jesus Christ has given to the Catholic Church. As indicated above, this goes back to a biblical account when our Lord Jesus Christ said to Peter, the first pope: 'you are Peter, and on this rock I will build my Church, and the gates of Hades shall not prevail against it. I will give you the keys of the kingdom of heaven, whatever you bind on earth shall be bound in heaven; and whatever you loose on earth shall be loosed in heaven' (Mt 16:18–19).

The Need for Baptised Christians to Go to Confession

What a great spiritual gift from the hands of St Peter to the succeeding popes who ordained others from one generation to the other and then to the present generation, giving them the opportunity to provide the spiritual needs specially to the baptised Christians, as well as show the light to other members of the different communities in the world from time immemorial!

So, as clearly indicated above, everyone in the house, particularly the baptised among them, need the spiritual boost gained by going to confessions and participating actively in the family devotions taking place under the leadership of the father, and sometimes by the mother, all in a bid to strengthen their faith and make themselves real soldiers of Christ. This gives some added boost to their spiritual engagements in the life of the universal Church, beginning from their local church.

The Sacrament of Confession

It cannot be over emphasised that the Catholic Church is blessed to have the sacrament of penance, or confession available to baptised Catholics who believe in their hearts that they have committed certain sins and therefore fallen short of God's grace. The fact that Catholics can have absolution for their sins speaks to the reality of why many Christians prefer to remain in the Catholic Church founded by Jesus Christ himself, as this helps them to put their relationship at right with God. It is found also that those who go to confession are always happy as they begin a new relationship with God, knowing too that Christ has made it abundantly clear to everyone that 'unless your righteousness exceeds that of the scribes and Pharisees, you will never enter into the kingdom of heaven' (Mt 5:20).

This calls on everyone to do his or her best to be righteous in whatever we do here on earth. So, with a functioning domestic church, a unique opportunity is provided to everyone to learn from the scriptures and the personal experiences of others on how to navigate through life as one faces different situations in life.

The privilege we have in listening to the experiences and testimonies of many Christians whether at home or in the parish Church goes a long way in educating us on how to navigate our own paths in life. In the process, we also learn a lot on how to keep the Ten Commandments in order to be in a good relationship with God for us to win eternal life at the end of our sojourn here on earth. Those who make great sacrifices to keep the Ten Commandments have the assurance that they will win eternal life because Jesus said: 'everyone who has left houses or brothers or sisters or father or mother or children or lands for my name's sake, will receive a hundredfold, and inherit eternal life' (Mt 19:29). If we all know this, it becomes clearer to all and sundry in the domestic church that father, mother, children, house-help, visitor, etc., all need to surrender himself or herself completely to Jesus Christ and obey God's commandments faithfully.

And once we are in Jesus' hands, it becomes quite easy for us to keep the Ten Commandments. This is when one really discovers that it is impossible for us to climb the ladder of holiness if we do not allow Jesus Christ to be the one directing and leading us to where we need to go, especially as regards our vocation and what we do for our living from day to day. So, for us not to be weighed down or think about discontinuing our daily struggle to climb the ladder of holiness, we need to come to Jesus every day to refresh ourselves. This is what many good Catholics do every day as they attend Holy Mass to receive Holy Communion and/or visit the Blessed Sacrament to pour out their hearts to our Lord and Saviour, Jesus Christ.

Leaving Our Burdens With Christ

Many Catholics have taken this as a task they must fulfil on a daily basis because Christ himself lovingly invites us to come to him when he says: 'Come to me, all who labour and are heavy laden, and I will give you rest. Take my yoke upon you, and learn from me, for I am gentle and lowly in heart, and you will find rest for your souls. For my yoke is easy and my burden light' (Mt 11:28–30). This constant refreshment from Jesus Christ emboldens us to take giant strides upwards on the ladder of holiness.

It is therefore appropriate to emphasise here that in this journey of faith where we have the opportunity to have our Lord Jesus Christ with us, we must not waste time to learn much from him with a view to applying his principles when many difficult situations rear their ugly heads. Whenever the situation in our hands turns ugly in spite of our attempts to be upright, we should always reflect in our hearts this problem-solving message that Jesus Christ has left with us and which should reverberate in our hearts everyday as we call upon him to save us. For us to find enduring rest, which Jesus himself also describes as the peace that this world cannot give, we must, like Jesus, be gentle and humble of heart.

Visible Acts of Generosity

In spite of Jesus' gentleness and humility, he faced a lot of suffering and persecution from his own people, even leading to a shameful death, a death on the cross. Before his death, he reached out to people from all walks of life, bringing the good news to them mainly in parables, but taking a good deal of his precious time to explain things in great detail to his Apostles to whom he would entrust the great mission of looking after his sheep. It was not surprising therefore that Jesus called on Peter three times, instructing him each time with these words: 'Feed my lambs', 'Tend my sheep', 'Feed my sheep' (Jn 21:15–17).

Joined with this unique duty of bringing the Good News to his people were Jesus' visible acts of genuine kindness and generosity to people of different categories of life. He went about everywhere doing good. It is these acts of generosity and readiness to face trials, persecution and even death that Jesus Christ requires us to learn from.

Our ability to hold on to our faith in the face of mounting challenges, trials, persecution, insults, gossip, etc., is what gives us the necessary push to climb the ladder of holiness. As we take great strides towards moving from one rung of the ladder to the next, be sure as human beings, many temptations will come our way. Many of these temptations we can resist if we are steadfast in prayer. But if through our own greed or selfishness, we fall into sin, we find ourselves climbing down the ladder of holiness. To remedy the situation, we must immediately go to confess our sins to an ordained Catholic priest, who in the power of our Lord Jesus Christ, can grant absolution of our sins.

After that, we should go to our quiet corner to say the prayers that the priest has mandated us to say in true repentance for our sins. In addition to these prayers, we could open up our bibles and say the following short prayers:

(a) Have mercy on me, O God, according to your merciful love; according to your abundant mercy blot out my transgressions. Wash me thoroughly from my iniquity, and cleanse me from my sin (Ps 51:1–2).

(b) Create in me a new heart, O God, and put a new and right spirit within me. Cast me not away from your presence, and take not your holy Spirit from me. Restore to me the joy of your salvation, and uphold me with a willing spirit (Ps 51:10–12).

(c) Lord, preserve my life, for I am godly; save your servant who trusts in you. You are my God; have mercy on me, O Lord, for to you I cry all day ... Give ear O Lord, to my prayer; listen to my cry of supplication. In the day of my trouble I called on you, for you do answer me (Ps 86:2–3, 6–7).

In this spiritual journey, we must not forget that Jesus listens to his Mother attentively. So, we must always ask our Mother Mary to intercede for us, remembering that it was the respect and honour that Jesus accords to his Mother that prompted his first miracle of turning water into wine at the Wedding Feast in Cana (Jn 2:5–10). Our Mother Mary did not even look back when she told the stewards: 'Do whatever he tells you' (Jn 2:5). This same virtue of obedience is what we must take along with us when climbing the ladder of holiness. Any disobedience, commitment of sin and/or our own disposition towards sinful acts, can, as indicated earlier, fling us back to the bottom rung of the ladder, just like the snake bite in a ludo game.

Another virtue we cannot afford to leave behind is that of faithfulness. Our faith and trust in God must not be shaken by threat. They must be total, unquestionable and unshakeable. Jesus himself speaks to us every day as he says: 'Let not your hearts be troubled; believe in God and believe also in me' (Jn 14:1).

Upholding Our Family Values

Be that as it may, we must always remember St Paul's advice to the Corinthians and to ourselves: 'Be watchful, stand firm in your faith, be courageous, be strong. Let all that you do be done in love' (1 Cor 16:13–14).

From what has been stated above, we can see that there is a continuous need to refresh ourselves in this journey of faith. We must renew our baptismal promises from time to time. Going to adult catechism classes sometimes is vital for our spiritual growth. This should be followed by faith-building retreats as well as family and leadership formation activities, seminars, workshops and conferences on subjects that have to do with human life, marriage and family spirituality.

During the adult catechism classes, one should also go through the basic fundamentals of Christian life, studying family values, and how to put into practice the virtues of Jesus, Mary and Joseph, the Holy Family of Nazareth. A separate course should be taught on how to avoid evils that could lead to grievous sins.

The study of the Ten Commandments of God, the rules and regulations of the Church, the Catholic social teachings as well as the Christian values that have come down to us from the time of the Apostles should all be in the front burners of the course. It is the knowledge gained from all these, in addition to the basic family values one has learnt from home that will create the urgently needed spiritual revolution in our families. Such a revolution will dissuade many from sinful acts, such as the sins of abortion, assassination, corruption, adultery/flirtation, armed robbery, divorce, culpable deceit, unnecessary displays of nudity in public, female breast-harassment, etc.

It is only when members of the household of God avoid these evil practices that they can be in good standing with God for he warns us daily as he speaks to us, saying: 'Amend your ways and your doings and I will let you dwell in this place. Do not trust in their deceptive words: "This is the temple of the Lord, the temple of the Lord, the temple of the Lord". For if you truly amend your ways and your doings, if you truly execute justice one with another, if you do not oppress the alien, the fatherless or the widow, or shed innocent blood in this place, and if you do not go after other gods to your own hurt, then I will let you dwell in this place, in the land that I gave of old to your fathers forever' (Jer 7:3–7).

Avoiding the Occasions of Sin

In conclusion, it should be clear to all and sundry by now that it is the courage and the wisdom one displays in avoiding any occasion of sin that can take us higher up the ladder of holiness. Any sinful act always takes one down the ladder of holiness. When one cherishes to be on the upward climb of this ladder of holiness, one must not look back; instead, one is to be steadfast in prayer while keeping to God's commandments and following the rules and regulations of the Church. One should also make it a point of duty to read the bible every day to deepen one's faith, join at least one pious society, such as the Holy Family Society, that will help one grow spiritually with family members and with people of the same faith, practise acts of generosity as well as attend to the poorest of the poor, coupled with meeting one's responsibility at home, in the Church, to the nation, and to the world at large.

No one can do all these by his or her own power. We need God's help, hence he said: 'Ask and it will be given to you; seek and you will find; knock and it will be opened to you. For everyone who asks, receives, and he who seeks finds and him who knocks it will be opened' (Mt 7:7–8). This is what God has assured us of, and we should not waver in making an appropriate request to him, especially as we already know that it is with his help that we can truly climb the ladder of holiness with integrity and honour. It is only when we do this that we can then expect to arrive safely in heaven.

Using the Domestic Church for Our Own Spiritual Benefits

Having discovered what it takes to climb the ladder of holiness, it is quite appropriate to conclude here that if the domestic church is made very functional, it has a substantial role to play in prompting family members to climb the ladder of holiness to eternal glory. Let us all therefore courageously make good use of the domestic church for our own spiritual benefits, because there is a great probability that a number of saints in the making are among those who are alive and kicking today, a number of them we may have passed by on the road, boarded the same flight with, attended the same Mass with, dined together with in the same restaurant, etc. One of such saints could be yourself. It is time to think about it.

Holy Family: Make our family like yours!

Jesus, Mary and Joseph: Protect our family and save the souls of all the faithful departed!

Holy Family: Be our model and our inspiration!

4

Domestic Church:
A Place to Grow in Family Holiness

In the scriptures, we learn that 'a man is justified by faith apart from the works of law' (Rm 3:28). To help understand this, St Paul who made this declaration asked a rhetorical question to which he also provided an answer. First, he posed the question: 'Do we then overthrow the Law by this faith?'. Answering this question himself, he said: 'By no means. On the contrary, we uphold the Law' (Rm 3:31).

For his listeners not to miss the message he was propounding, St Paul made it clear that the Law has nothing to do with putting people in the right relationship with God. He pointed out that 'the righteousness of God has been manifested apart from the Law, although the Law and the Prophets bear witness to it' (Rm 3:21). Continuing, he said that we can only see the righteousness of God 'through faith in Jesus Christ for all who believe' (Rm 3:22). St Paul's spiritual affirmation is seen as a guide to all Christians and non-Christians alike who are desirous of working towards holiness in the family.

St Matthew Clarifies the Message of God

To ensure that no one makes any mistake about this, it is also important for family members who are determined to learn more about the scriptures from the comfort of their homes and/or in the Church to find time to read St Matthew's Gospel on the same subject.

St Matthew succinctly explained that it is not only to obey the commandments of God that are simply called the law, but to also teach them. He emphasised in Matthew 5:19 that: 'whoever then relaxes one of the least of these commandments and teaches men so, shall be called least in the kingdom of heaven but he who does them and teaches them shall be called great in the kingdom of heaven'.

Having taken note of these very important passages in the bible, it becomes the business of the head of a family to consciously mobilise his household to give proper meaning to the message that both St Paul and St Matthew have conveyed to us in order to have a good start in the struggle to put our faith in Jesus Christ into practice.

Attributing the Correct Meaning to the Word of God

Quite often we receive God's message, which we are not able to decipher quickly, or we simply ignore without any attempt to decipher the meaning of the words spoken to us. This happens to every human being. But those who welcome God's message into their hearts, spend some time to decipher such a message, and then act upon it like St Joseph in the bible, always rejoice throughout their lives for doing so. For us to understand clearly how to listen to God's word and act upon it, we need to consider here the example given to us by St Joseph as recorded in Matthew 1:18–25. In summary, Mary, the wife of Joseph had been betrothed to him, before they came to live together as husband and wife. 'She was found to be with child of the Holy Spirit; and her husband Joseph, being a just man, and unwilling to put her to shame resolved to send her away quietly. But as he considered this, behold an angel of the Lord appeared to him in a dream, saying, "Joseph, son of David do not fear to take Mary your wife, for that which is conceived in her is of the Holy Spirit; she will bear a son and you shall call his name Jesus, for he will save his people from their sins." ... When Joseph woke up from sleep, he did as the angel of the Lord commanded him; he took his wife, but knew her not until she had born a son and he called his name Jesus'.

This is what it means to receive God's word, ruminate over it and then act upon it in a positive manner. Unfortunately, many people in the world do not follow this example of St Joseph. It is this refusal to listen to God's word that has brought wars and tribulations to the world. We find that the many evils of abortion, suicide, armed robbery, ritual killings, embezzlement of public funds, snatching of husbands or wives, internet fraud, etc., are being committed in different parts of the world because those who received God's word into their hearts refused to act upon it in a positive manner. Instead, they preferred to do their own biddings, which unfortunately present evil and destructive acts to the world.

It is for us not be contributors to evil acts that the almighty God gave us St Joseph as a good example for us to always imitate. It is his virtues of obedience and self-abandonment to God's will that family members are expected to learn from and strive to put into practice in our daily activities. Christians are to understand clearly that when we receive God's word either as it is written in the scriptures, delivered into our hearts by an angel of God (as in the case of Joseph), spoken to us by an anointed priest of God from the pulpit, or through our interactions with other people, we need quiet time to decipher the message in order to attribute the correct meaning to it. And once the message is clear in one's heart, then one still needs to come to Jesus, imploring him to grant one the wisdom, the strength and the courage to act decisively on God's message. Anyone who goes through this route in attending to both private and public issues will find joy and peace dwelling in his or heart.

Our individual experiences of this, on waiting on Jesus to send the Holy Spirit to direct us in our various actions would fill tens of books if they were to be compiled. And if we were to compile the instances when we ignored God's message and instead did our own bidding, we would find too that hundreds of books could also be turned out as a result of this. Our forefathers in faith experienced this also, hence they looked out for the coming of Christ into the world to help give them a new direction. And when Christ came into the world, he didn't mind the background of those he met, but selected twelve out of them to be used for God's purpose on earth.

What should immediately come to our mind here is that over two thousand years ago, Christ selected twelve Apostles for his three-year mission on earth, who had similar experiences of not understanding God's messages correctly. It was because of this that Christ lovingly 'opened their minds to understand the scriptures' (Lk 24:45) since they showed a lack of understanding of what he taught them, especially when he used parables to deliver his messages.

The Catholic Church's Position on Revelations

The above presupposes that scriptural passages are not what we can easily attribute ordinary meanings to in our day-to-day living. There are always many things that would come to our minds while in the process of discerning the message. The circumstances that propelled the message, the elements used in conveying the message, the local customs and traditions of the people to whom the message is addressed, the place where the message was delivered, etc., are some of the factors that come to one's mind that can either blur or aid the discernment of the message. But what comes out clearly in this process of discernment, is that we see the great need for allowing the Holy Spirit to teach and guide us to 'all the truth' about the messages we receive from time to time. Jesus told his Apostles, and this is a message for all of us, that: 'I have yet many things to say to you but you cannot hear them now. When the spirit of truth comes, he will guide you into all the truth; for he will not speak on his own authority, but whatever he hears, he will speak and he will declare to you the things that are to come' (Jn 16:12–13).

It is when we have such experiences with the Holy Spirit that we can say that our minds have been opened to the correct interpretations of what we read from the bible, from the commentaries and reflections of scriptural scholars; from the internet; what we hear in homilies, from the pulpit and/or hear in God's word from other people in our daily interactions in society. The same Holy Spirit empowers us, inspires us and encourages us to act on the messages. In addition to these interpreted messages are those we also receive through apparitions, many a time leaving us with messages we cannot easily understand.

The Catholic Church is aware that we periodically receive revelations, hence she made it abundantly clear in the Catechism of the Catholic Church, Paragraph 67, that 'Throughout the ages, there have been so-called "private" revelations, some of which have been recognised by the authority of the Church. They do not belong, however to the deposit of faith ... Guided by the Magisterium of the Church, the sensus fidelium knows how to discern and welcome in these revelations whatever constitutes an authentic call of Christ or his saints to the Church'. It goes further to emphasise that 'Christian faith cannot accept "revelations" that claim to surpass or correct the Revelation of which Christ is the fulfilment'.

Creating a Conducive Atmosphere for Evangelisation

Knowing that we need the Holy Spirit to guide us to the complete truth as regards the meaning of the Word of God, it becomes advantageous to have a domestic church where prayers are said regularly together. It is also beneficial to have the opportunity to share the Word of God among the participants while some more experienced people present there could make their own efforts to explain what they understand from the texts that have been read. It therefore becomes crucial for the father of the home to take major steps along with his wife to create a conducive atmosphere where all members of the family will consciously prepare themselves to put right their relationship with God. This is quite important since 'the righteousness of God has been manifested apart from the law, although the Law and the Prophets bear witness to it' (Rm 3:21). Is there any wonder that this more or less makes it mandatory for good Christian families to always have well organised, spiritually-motivated and faith-building encounters with God in their spiritual activities? Once a conducive atmosphere is established and a place within the home is designated for daily/weekly family devotion, it becomes quite easy too for everyone in the home to take necessary steps to join others who are ready to develop their faith in Jesus Christ.

The question that should arise here is: why do people need to develop their faith? This is undoubtedly a crucial question but it can be easily answered by making some references to the scriptures. To begin with, one can make three leading statements that will help to unravel the answer to this question. They are:

(a) God so loved the world that he sent his only beloved Son to this world to show us that he is 'the Way, the Truth and the Life' (Jn 14:6), and to die for our sins.

(b) After Christ's baptism, the Spirit of God descended from heaven like a dove to reveal him as the Son of God saying: 'This is my beloved Son, with whom I am well pleased' (Mt 3:17).

(c) In Nazareth, where Jesus grew up, he went into the temple and read a passage from the scroll of the Prophet Isaiah where it is written thus: 'The Spirit of the Lord is upon me, because he has anointed me to preach good news to the poor. He has sent me to proclaim release to the captives and recovering of sight to the blind, to set at liberty those who are oppressed, to proclaim the acceptable year of the Lord'. And after reading this, he said: 'Today this scripture has been fulfilled in your hearing' (Lk 4:17–21).

From the three scriptural texts that are referred to above, one can see the reasonableness of building our faith in Jesus Christ. In addition to God's revelation of Jesus Christ's identity, Christ also found a good occasion to reveal the relationship between the almighty God and himself to his disciples when he said: 'I am the true vine and my

Father is the vinedresser. Every branch that bears no fruit, he takes away, and every branch that does bear fruit, he prunes, that it may bear more fruit' (Jn 15:1–2). And for all to receive this message clearly, Christ emphasised that: 'If you abide in me and my words abide in you, ask whatever you will and it shall be done for you' (Jn 15:7).

Considering this promise from the only begotten Son of God, it is only wise and proper that we build our faith in him. The beginning point must be from the home because every good thing begins from the home and it is what we have learned in the home that we can exhibit in public.

Should anyone still have any doubt as to why an essential part of the Holy Family Society's spirituality programme is centred on the home, with a view to revamping and revitalising the domestic church? We believe that if there were certain questions before as to why the society was redirecting people back to the home and to jealously uphold our extended family system, the recent worldwide lockdown due to the coronavirus pandemic has brought some good news along with the deadly virus, to clear any doubt and further stress the fact that it was high time our domestic churches functioned effectively. Let families therefore put their homes in order by creating a conducive environment for the domestic churches to thrive in with active participation of members of their households.

As already indicated earlier, it is necessary that parents in the home take the lead, as their own firm resolve and discipline can show the way, especially in taking the necessary actions to begin their family devotion, for instance, by tomorrow, i.e., if, they can make up their minds today. All they need to do is to inform everyone in the house that the family prayer meeting begins at a specified time, morning or evening as the case may be, so that everyone is aware. If in the end, it is only the parents and one child or one family relation that are present for the prayers, the convener should count himself or herself blessed, as the almighty God has assured us that: 'where two or three are gathered in my name, there am I in the midst of them' (Mt 18:20).

So, to see that people have a good start, it is the responsibility of both parents to ensure that members of the household are not only present for the family devotion but also participate actively in the reading and sharing of the scriptural passages. As part of the package, a little time should always be given for private reflection after the sharing. All the participants are expected to profit spiritually from the family devotion, which should take place either in the designated private chapel or in a sacred place that is daily arranged for that purpose in the home, thereby making the domestic church quite functional.

Modelling Our Lives After Jesus, Mary and Joseph

A keen student of the bible will discover that early Christian families who had to come together in the way suggested above allocated quality time in their homes to family prayers. This was part of their day-to-day activities in their effort to model their lives after Jesus, who taught them, especially his disciples, how to pray. This example of our forefathers in faith is what we all need to take to our domestic church in order to give credence to our desire to work our way to holiness while still here on earth, and then to sainthood.

Families will also discover that God himself gave us the model family of Jesus, Mary and Joseph, the Holy Family of Nazareth who we must endeavour to imitate in our individual families. Those who take this seriously will eventually discover that if they give due honour to Jesus, Mary and Joseph, they will have taken a holy and desirable step to put their family members in the right relationship with God. This, of course, is only revealed to those who have faith in Christ and constantly read his signals in the horizon.

For us to know how to navigate our spiritual paths, without having divided minds, Christ himself specifically speaks to us: 'Let not your hearts be troubled; believe in God, believe also in me' (Jn 14:1).

Jesus Is the Way to Our Heavenly Home

Having taken note of this, the father of the home who leads the domestic church should take the initiative from the beginning to dialogue with his wife before any announcement to the people living with them about going on a joint spiritual journey. It is, no doubt, a thing of great joy to take every member of the household to Christ. This is what many would love to do, but there is always some difficultly, because of the different schedules of the people in the home, for resuming work in their offices or business sites or for the children to begin their classes in school.

However, a decision could be taken to choose the time acceptable for most people in the home. This will mean setting up a particular time when it is most convenient for everyone to congregate for family devotion. If the married couples remember how they planned their honeymoon together immediately after their marriage celebrations or how they planned their first visit to Disney World in Florida, USA together, or to any place outside their home for an unprecedented 'chill out' break, they should be able to plan joyfully on how to make their family devotion more effective and pleasing to God. To get everyone highly motivated to join the family devotion, the father and mother of the children would need to, first and foremost, create a conducive atmosphere where there is love, peace and harmony in the home. They may also be required to make necessary sacrifices to purchase certain furniture items, altar cloths, candle stands, flower vessels, musical instruments, light installations, etc., to induce a prayerful environment at any time the family members come together for the devotion. Such efforts help tremendously to establish a thriving domestic church. All that is important thereafter is to help all to understand the spiritual benefits accruable to all members of the household if they remain regular devotees to the family devotion.

The message that should be distributed is simple: that there is great joy here on earth and unimaginable spiritual rewards in heaven for family members who pray together with a view to building their faith in Jesus Christ who is 'the Way' to our Father in heaven. In so doing, it becomes much easier for family members to learn how to put into practice all that they learn about Jesus, his mother, Mary and his foster father, Joseph. And once this becomes the daily practice of the participants in the activities of the domestic church, they will find themselves already at a good start in their spiritual journey that will hopefully take them through the narrow road to our real home in heaven.

If this message sells well to everyone in the household, they must also be made to know that they cannot go empty handed on this spiritual journey. They must equip themselves with certain fundamentals that have been designed by God to make such a faith-building venture quite successful. These fundamentals are what I will draw the reader's attention to in the next chapter. Please be prepared to embark on this very important spiritual journey with what has been recommended in the next chapter. There are essential spiritual tools that pilgrims going on this life-saving pilgrimage should pay particular attention to as they are all essentials for one's luggage to make the journey from one's earthly home worthwhile and pleasantly successful. They help to determine whether one is really set to lay a solid spiritual foundation for his or her own home. It is only when one has built his or her home on a solid foundation that one can help other family members, friends and/or associates to set up theirs.

It is quite reassuring that those who have built their homes on solid rock, which is Jesus Christ himself, and whose name is above every other name, will find joy as they move along the narrow road to heaven. Christians must understand that 'there is salvation in no one else' apart from Jesus, 'for there is no other name under heaven given among men by which we must be saved' (Acts 4:12).

5

Domestic Church as Catalyst for Making Saints Out of Our Families!

From the inception of the Holy Family Society, its spiritual programmes have been deliberately focused on sainthood with a view to getting its members to cherish the idea of growing in holiness and advancing their family spirituality. The reason, as explained in the preceding chapter, is that as all canonised saints who were once in this world came from different families, there are great possibilities that families on earth can still produce holy men and women who could be canonised in the future.

Our concept is that if this is continuously driven into the consciousness of families, more and more people in different parts of the world, whether they are members of the Holy Family Society or not, will be more determined to do a number of 'ordinary things in an extraordinary manner' that could eventually make the Church consider some of them for beatification and/or canonisation.

This has therefore been a special goal of the Holy Family Society, which we hold very dear, and is specifically designed to encourage family members all over the world to work towards holiness.

Married Laypersons as Saints in the Catholic Church
From the records of the Catholic Church, it is highly encouraging to observe that four married laypersons have been canonised as saints since the year 1622.

They are:

(a) St Isidore Merlo Quintana and Blessed Maria Torribia de la Cabeza Merlo. Maria Torribia herself (although beatified) has not yet been canonised. Both Isidore and his wife, Maria Torribia, were said to have had one son who 'fell into a deep well, and at the prayers of his parents, the water of the well is said to have risen miraculously to the level of the ground', bringing the child up to be picked.[1] With so many other miracles to his credit, totalling up to 438, Isidore, who was born in 1070 (no particular date recorded), was canonised in Rome on 12 March 1622, by Pope Gregory XV. His feast day is 15 May, the day he died in 1130.

(b) Sts Louis Aloys Martin (1823–94) and Marie-Azélie Guérin Martin (1831–77) were married from the Diocese of Séez and Bayeux-Lisieux (France).

(c) Servant of God Pietro Molla (1912-2010) and St Gianna Beretta Molla (1922–62) were also married laypersons from the Archdiocese of Milan in Italy.

Married Persons as Blessed, Venerable and Servants of God in the Catholic Church

It is to be noted that three married couples have been declared as Blessed in the Catholic Church.

They are:

(a) Blesseds Luigi Beltramme Quattrocchi (1880–1951) and Maria Corsini-Beltrame Quattrocchi (1884–1965) from the Vicariate of Rome. They were beatified on 21 October 2001 by Pope St John Paul II. Their feast day is 25 November.

---

[1] Michael Ott, *The Catholic Encyclopedia*, Vol. 8, 'St Isidore the Labourer', New York: Robert Appleton Company, http://www.newadvent.org/cathen/08189a.htm; accessed 19 Sept 2021.

(b) Blessed Karl I (IV) von Osterreich (1887–1922) and Servant of God Zita de Bourbon-Parma (1892–1989). They were from the Archdiocese of Vienna and the Diocese of Le Mans; they were Emperor and Empress of Austria-Hungary (Portugal-Italy-Switzerland-Austria).

(c) Blessed Bartolo Longo (1841–1926) and Marianna Farnararo de Fusco Longo (1836–1924). They were from the Diocese of Pompeii and were members of the lay Dominicans as well as the founders of the Dominican Sisters of Pompeii in Italy.

It should also be of great interest to all Catholics that the Church has also graciously declared two married couples as Venerable.

They are:

(a) Venerable Pierre Toussaint (1766–1853) and Servant of God Juliette Noel Toussaint (*c.* 1786–1851). Both were of the Archdiocese of New York. The husband was originally from Haiti while the wife was from United States of America.

(b) Venerables Sergio Bernardini (1882–1966) and Domenica Bedonni Bernardini (1889–1971). They were a married couple from the Archdiocese of Modena-Nonatola who were also members of the secular Franciscans in Italy.

There are thirty-five other laypersons since the thirteenth century who have been declared, as at the time of writing this book, as Servants of God by the Church. Those who have been listed as candidates for sainthood number thirty-six. It should also be of great relevance to mention here that when the process for the beatification of Luigi Beltrame Quattrocchi and his wife, Maria Corsini-Beltrame Quattrocchi was validated on 20 June 1997, the Prefect of the Congregation for the Causes of Saints, Cardinal José Saraiva Martins, remarked that the couple 'made a true domestic church of their family, which was open to life, prayer, the social apostolate, solidarity with the poor and friendship'.[2]

Having more or less given us an exposé of what married persons should concern themselves with while still alive, it has been my prayer that the remark of this Cardinal, coming from the Vatican, should fire up married persons throughout the world, especially Catholic couples who have wholeheartedly received the message of Christ and the universal call to holiness, to make the necessary amends in their lives to enable them to follow the footsteps of the Quattrocchis so that they themselves will receive the crown of glory at the end of their sojourn in this world.

'Make Saints Out of Your Family' – A Slogan of the Holy Family Society

It is equally important to note here that Pope Benedict XVI, during his pontificate, awarded Papal honours in the category of Knighthood to women in 2005. This greatly enhanced the status of practising and helpful married women in the Church. There was no doubting the fact that those who received such an honour had for years conscientiously and steadfastly worked for the good of humanity and the Church. This is why, since 2005, we have had cases where husbands and wives have been separately honoured as Papal Knights, and in some cases, only the wives of Catholic men were considered for such a great honour in the Church. The awards of Papal Knighthood of St Gregory the Great and of St Sylvester to lay married couples in the Catholic Church are highly appreciative and encouraging.

As we thank God for this development, the Holy Family Society is not resting on its oars in honouring men and women who lived in this world and have been canonised as saints in the Catholic Church. Every year, on the 1 November, a date which the Church has set aside

---

[2] *EWTN*, 'Bl Luigi Beltrame Quattrocchi and Bl Maria Corsini', https://www.ewtn.com/catholicism/library/bl-luigi-beltrame-quattrocchi-and-bl-maria-corsini-5630; accessed 19 September 2021.

for the celebration of the Solemnity of All Saints, the Holy Family Society has adopted a general theme: 'Make Saints Out of Your Family' for a four-day celebration. This celebration gives an ample opportunity to get all to become focused on holiness and sainthood. The spiritual exercises the participants undertake during the celebrations act as catalysts to boost their family spirituality. With the spiritual programmes, the participants stand to gain a lot if they take to heart the need to strive on daily basis to put what they have learnt into practice and live holy lives. They are also told the benefits of getting members of one's family to continue the daily struggle of obeying God's commandments as well as observing the rules and regulations of the Church.

Apart from these initiatives, the Holy Family Society also encourages its members and all Christians and non-Christians alike to read its spiritually inspiring books, all of which give credence to the fact that everything God created in this world is good and the elements therefrom are divinely oriented, and if given sacred interpretation they could be used as instruments to advance knowledge and climb the ladder of holiness. Our Lord Jesus Christ carried this out effectively during his three-year mission on earth as he employed various elements that the people were already familiar with to deliver his life-giving messages.

Reading Good Spiritual Books
Since everything God created in this world is good, we should therefore study the good things in our culture, especially the elements we hold so dear. We should attribute good meanings to them and use them for our spiritual development. This will help in our inculturation and our advancement towards holiness. All that should be uppermost in our mind at all times is to continuously use every occasion in our life and all the good things that God makes available to us every day for our spiritual development to thank and honour him. No one should look back while doing this.

To help its members to stay on top of this, the Holy Family Society has taken it as its onerous task to regularly direct the attention of all to relevant, soul-captivating passages in the bible that should constantly act as a guide to everyone through which we could all be further inspired, not only to promote our family and Christian values, but also to improve our relationship with our God.

This explains why the Holy Family Society happily takes the initiative to recommend a number of other books that could act as catalysts to motivate its members to continuously ascend the ladder of holiness. Such books and motivational artworks are being regularly exhibited by the society for interested families to buy and use for their own spiritual benefits.

Apart from this, the Holy Family Society has two WhatsApp National platforms onto which a number of spiritual reflections and homilies delivered during daily Masses are posted to further educate members as well as help them with their reflections and sharing in their domestic churches. Since the society has more than seven members of its Council of Priests and Religious posting their daily reflections and/or homilies on our WhatsApp National Platforms, it has become much easier for family members to share the Word of God during their family devotion in the comfort of their homes. It has also been easier for some of them to take free time off in their office to share some of the spiritual reflections on their WhatsApp platforms with some members of their staff, giving opportunities to many who consciously make the necessary sacrifices every day to improve their family spirituality and grow in holiness.

The Two Invisible Ladders
Our findings, however, have revealed that there are a few members who do not read spiritually inspired books and are not so much concerned about climbing the ladder of holiness. What seemed to have been in vogue for most people in the world before the coronavirus pandemic came to teach everyone a hard lesson, was the

urge usually created by sinful thoughts and actions that led many to climb the ladder of darkness.

Why do many people have this urge for evil and crime, you may wonder? It is because people are bombarded, almost twenty-four hours a day through telephone, emails, fax, radio, television, newspapers, magazines, online unsolicited messages, etc., with information, over 75 per cent of which is meant to focus one's attention toward the frivolous things of this world. Unfortunately, such material creates earthly joy as well as evil inclinations to amass wealth and deprive others of their goods and positions for personal benefits at the expense of eternal bliss. One of the persuasive arguments often spread throughout social media includes the assertion that if no one here on earth can guarantee what is really awaiting one after death, why should one worry about the unknown? And so, many people are swept off their feet after reading or hearing such arguments. They thereafter begin to care less about their souls and what happens to them after their demise. This is why there is a daily multiplication of crimes in the world, all resulting from the soul-contaminating publications and broadcasts through electronic media and online messages through the internet.

What is paramount for us to understand is that from the day we attain the age of reasoning, two ladders are placed before us; one, the ladder of holiness to make our way back to heaven, where there is eternal bliss, the other, the ladder of darkness that could lead those who have signed up with the devil to have their own freedom to move on foolishly to hellfire, where there is eternal fire and the gnashing of teeth.

These two ladders are placed side by side for us to decide which one to climb. Everyone is expected to be independent with the fundamental freedom to make his or her own choice. But there are some people who have sold the freedom given to them on a platter of gold, and so find themselves being foolishly led to begin a new journey on the ladder of darkness. This is quite unfortunate.

As the Holy Family Society's preoccupation is to concern itself with encouraging people to have a strong faith in Jesus as they progress on their ladder of holiness, our main focus in this chapter is to primarily give an exposé, as it were, on how family members can effectively achieve this with the help of our Lord Jesus Christ who has promised to be with us until the end of time.

To reassure us that he will not abandon those who place their trust in him, Christ says to us every day that: 'If you abide in me and my words abide in you, ask whatever you will and it shall be done for you. By this my Father is glorified, that you bear much fruit, and so prove to be my disciples' (Jn 15:7–8). Having known this, all we need is to ask him on a daily basis to grant us the grace and the strength for our continuous climb on the rungs of the ladder of holiness.

Let it be made clear here that the ladder of holiness is the ladder of life. One needs to know that it is this same ladder of holiness and life that our Lord Jesus Christ directs our attention to when he says to us every day: 'I am the Way, the Truth, and the Life; no one comes to the Father but through me' (Jn 14:6).

Climbing the Spiritual Ladder of Jesus Christ

Jesus gives us a clear indication that we can climb this ladder of holiness to reach the narrow road, which will lead us to the Way that will finally take us to our Father in heaven. This why he gives himself to us every day as a special gift in Holy Communion, announcing that those who learn of him, lean on him, eat his body and drink his blood, as they faithfully do his Father's will here on earth, will definitely make it to heaven, where he himself has prepared mansions for the righteous.

Apart from the assurance we have from our Lord Jesus Christ that the righteous will make it to heaven, our almighty God himself assured us from time immemorial that a place has been prepared for those who do his holy will, when he said: 'Behold, I send an angel before you, to guard you on the way, and to bring you to the place which I have prepared. Give heed to him and listen to his voice, do not rebel against him for he will not pardon your transgressions; for my name is in him. But if you listen attentively to his voice, and all that I say, then, I will be an enemy to your enemies and an adversary to your adversaries' (Ex 23:20–22).

So, if we do not falter in serving our all-loving God, he further assures thus: 'I will bless your bread and your water; and I will take sickness away from the midst of you. None shall cast her young or be barren in your land; I will fulfil the number of your days. I will send my terror before you, and will throw into confusion all the people against whom you shall come, and I will make all your enemies turn their backs to you (Ex 23:25–27).

From the foregoing, it should not surprise anyone that the Psalmist also gave those who place their complete trust in God a comforting assurance that: 'Because you have made the Lord your refuge, the Most High your habitation, no evil shall befall you, nor scourge come to your tent' (Ps 91:9–10). For us to know that God has deployed his angels to be in charge of our lives, the Psalmist further informed us thus: 'For he will give his angels charge of you to guard you in all your ways' (Ps 91:11).

One can therefore state here without any iota of doubt, that it was in relying on and trusting in the promises of God that the holy men and women of old made their way to heaven. And those whom the Church has so far canonised as saints deservedly gained entrance into heaven because they followed Christ's footsteps and clung firmly to him while they were here on earth. This is what the scriptures and the Church have confirmed to us in so many ways. And on our own, we can read and understand; we can listen to sermons and assimilate the messages, all informing us that those who have been canonised as saints left their own footprints and remarkable legacies, to show us that in our present world the only way to salvation is to cling firmly to Jesus.

All we therefore need do is to read more about the saints and follow in their footsteps, imitating them as much as possible. We should also not be afraid to invite our own guardian angels and the Holy Spirit to make their presence felt within us as they deliver spiritual messages from God to us daily that are meant to direct our footsteps, lead us aright, protect us from the hands of the evil one, save us from all forms of danger as well as inspire us to be steadfast in our faith as we climb steadily the ladder of holiness during our sojourn here on earth.

What is quite remarkable to note at this point is that because our angels use this same ladder of holiness to come down from heaven to deliver spiritual messages to people, Jacob in his day was inspired by the Holy Spirit to speak thus about his dream at Bethel: 'there was a ladder set up on the earth and the top of it reached to heaven; and behold, the angels of God were ascending and descending on it' (Gn 28:12). And at a different occasion, Jesus himself told Nathanael in John 1:51: 'Truly, truly, I say to you, you will see heaven open and the angels of God ascending and descending upon the Son of man'. This indicates that the spiritual vehicle our angels use to descend and ascend is the spiritual ladder of holiness that holy men and women also use also to make their way to the narrow road. Our prayer therefore is for our Lord Jesus Christ to find us worthy to climb this same ladder of holiness to meet him who is 'the Way, the Truth and the Life' any time we are invited back to our permanent home in heaven.

Jesus the Way, the Truth and the Life
As it has been made abundantly clear to the reader in this chapter, Jesus, who is 'the Way, the Truth and the Life', graciously died for our sins to free us from our original sin so that, as free citizens, we can take our place at his table. What can one therefore say that our Lord Jesus Christ has not done for us? Do we really appreciate all of this?

Be that as it may, it should be interesting for us all to know that our own decision to follow Christ is what brings us to the first rung of the ladder. This comes when we present ourselves voluntarily, after rigorous spiritual exercises and/or experiences, for baptism to be administered on us, which completely washes our original sin away.

From that very moment, we are fully initiated into the Catholic Church through this same sacrament of baptism. We become fully-fledged members of God's household.

This is why Jesus himself assured us that as soon as we achieve this status, we should see ourselves as 'no longer strangers, and sojourners, but you are fellow citizens with the saints and members of the household of God' (Eph 2:19). Everyone should see this not only as good news but also as our Lord's inspiring words, which should create a spiritual revolution in us that will lead us to God. On this note, the curtain for this chapter is humbly lowered for the reader to ask some rhetorical questions, with a view to taking positive action for spiritual development.

6
_____

Human Life: What Value to Attach – Does Mine Have Meaning?

'Musings' by Most Rev. Dr Hilary Nanman Dachelem CMF
Catholic Bishop of Bauchi

This chapter highlights the essence of my reflections on the many topics concerning human life in the preceding two volumes of this book. It is important to note from the beginning that the main text of this chapter is a contribution from Most Rev. Dr Hilary Nanman Dachelem, CMF, Catholic Bishop of Bauchi. He permitted me to use the text in order to help families to reflect on the true meaning of life and why it is important to choose life instead of death.

It will be his joy to see many families devoting quality time to read this piece and thereafter resolving to always choose to serve God and humanity instead of mammon and money; to be at peace with the living God instead of dining and sleeping with Satan. He will also be happy to see that we are all in the bandwagon that promotes family life in the community, instead of being with the agents or cults that are hell-bent on destroying family life and/or its institutions.

The bishop points out clearly that for any human being to be in the company of those who are holding on firmly to our Lord, Jesus Christ as their personal Saviour, and also follow the narrow road with thorns and sufferings that leads to heaven, one needs to attribute the correct meaning to life. This must be borne in mind at every stage of our life, especially when making critical decisions about one's life. A keen reader of the bishop's 'musings' will discover that one cannot run away from the need to attribute the correct meaning to life if one really wants to make a success out of it and be in the right relationship with God.

In creating us as humans, the almighty God, in his infinite mercy and love, gave us freedom of choice, which he expects everyone to use positively in order to be at peace with him. It was for us to do this successfully that he specially created us in his image and likeness. Every human person therefore has the privilege to use his or her thinking faculty to decide what he or she wants in life.

It is true that in our growing years our parents decided a number of things for us, for example when to start school and what school to attend, when to be presented for infant baptism and when to begin our preparation classes for holy communion, etc. But as soon as we become adults, mainly from the age of eighteen upwards, everyone is expected to decide the course of his or her life. This shows that at particular periods in human life, crucial moments for decision making arrive for the young adult. Such periods include discerning the purpose for which God created one and what steps to take to fulfil the identified purpose during the course of our life.

This is not a subject to ignore as it is one of the crucial issues that confronts people daily, especially when there is no clear focus and there are signals that certain tasks are not being achieved as planned or there have been certain missing links in one's life. It is to help those who are overburdened with the task of understanding where to proceed from where they are at the moment, and to know what God is calling on them to do in life, that the subject: 'How Meaningful is "My Meaning"?', as expertly addressed by Bishop Hilary Nanman Dachelem, CMF, becomes relevant. The bishop has handled this subject so well that everyone will find the musings therein quite useful in determining the correct meaning of his or her life in order to reconstruct one's personal life, as it were, with the sole purpose of achieving what God had originally set out for one. In so doing, one will be able to help himself or herself to lay more emphasis on spiritual matters and make Christ be at the centre of one's day-to-day activities. It is only when people finally make their decision to always serve the living God that they become expectedly proficient in promoting and defending life and family with greater passion. This presupposes that the domestic church in such a home will be seen to be functioning at its best, with family members in a state of joy and happiness for serving the living God.

From the ongoing introduction to the subject the bishop is addressing herein, the reader will hopefully find his contribution, 'How Meaningful is "My Meaning"?', a useful piece to guide him or her on how to attribute meaning to what God is expecting him or her to do in life. I, having first read the script myself was convinced that any inquisitive mind who has probably read the first two volumes of this book may be set already to determine what God is expecting him or her to do in order to promote holiness in his or her family. In other words, the inquisitive reader of this book could very well use this opportunity to look into his or her individual life to see what he or she could do:

- to find the right course of life by attributing a sane and positive meaning to the reason why our benevolent God created him or her in his image and likeness.

- to discern the purpose for his or her creation and what level of achievements to be undertaken in this world before returning to the Lord.

- to discern the reason for his or her coming into the world through his or her own family.

- to find out what difference he or she could make in his or her family in getting everyone to move closer and closer to God for the purpose of winning eternal life at the end of everybody's sojourn here on earth.

- to understand what life generally means to him or her and what legacies he or she is expected to leave behind that can help to uplift the family spirituality of those in the family at the time of his or her exit from this world, etc.

These are some of the vital issues in one's life that family members who are concerned about their own faith and what life really means to them should be reflecting on regularly to be able to play their active roles in promoting and giving genuine spiritual life to a functioning domestic church.

I myself was very well agitated after reading the reflections of His Lordship on 'How Meaningful is "My Meaning"?'. Convinced that this will help a number of family members all over the world to find genuine reasons for their existence, I did not hesitate to request officially the permission of the bishop to publish his musings, and having been so granted, I now have the privilege to publish it below.

But before reading the musings, it is also good for the reader to have an insight into what led the bishop to reflect on this particular subject. Already, the reader must have noticed that this chapter itself is titled; 'Human Life: What Value to Attach – Does Mine Have Meaning?'

You may want to know that shortly after the coronavirus pandemic was foisted on the world, there was an alleged story of an Italian billionaire who was said to have committed suicide after he lost his family members through the same coronavirus, which had, at that point in time, killed several thousands of people throughout the world. This particular story spread around the world like wildfire. The then-trending news report was credited to a US based online channel, GoldMyne TV, which was said to have created the unverified video clip report that shocked the entire world. The tweet went viral with the following headline report:

> Italian billionaire commits suicide by throwing himself from the twentieth floor of his tower after his entire family was wiped out by coronavirus.

What made this report quite far-reaching was that several other users also shared the same video with the same message in Hindu and Indian languages. But on further enquiries, many found that there was an earlier claim indicating that the video was of a man from the US who committed suicide after he was diagnosed with the novel coronavirus. Another report that followed this claimed that it was a young boy in Italy who had committed the reported suicide after his family members died of coronavirus, but that the video clip, which was deceitfully shared along with the story was that of a previous suicide that had happened in Spain.

Although the different stories on the internet created a lot of confusion in the minds of many, what we took out of the different versions of the story up until today was that a human being created in the image and likeness of God died by suicide. This is why the reader will find below that the bishop began his musings by cautiously referring to the story as 'a purported case of an Italian billionaire'.

Not minding the confusion created by the stories, what was quite clear to all and sundry as indicated earlier was that a human life was involved. The video clip that went with the story showed a good number of people watching the man on a window on the twentieth floor of a building who stuck out his neck, shouting, and thereafter took a plunge as he dived down immediately to his death. This certainly prompted the bishop's musings below:

How Meaningful is "My Meaning"?
(Musings of Bishop Hilary Nanman Dachelem, CMF, Catholic Bishop of Bauchi on 'Meaning' in the world)

A Pathetic Scenario
There is a purported case of an Italian billionaire, who threw himself down from a twenty-storey building and killed himself after all the members of his family who died due to the Coronavirus, which kept taunting my mind with a lot of musings or reflections. When I read the story, I was taken aback. The event is very pathetic, sorrowful, quite devastating and deeply painful.

Questions Provoked by the Scenario

The above scenario provokes many reflections within me, provoking me to wonder a lot about life, its mysteries and complexities. The scenario further brings me to the following questions: what does a meaningful life mean? Or more basically, in what does meaning really consist? What does the word 'meaning' mean for different people? Can there be 'true meaning' among different meanings of a thing or event? If there is such a thing as true meaning, in what does it consist? What is it that makes life 'meaningful'?

The search for meaning is a journey that began thousands of years ago by philosophers, scientists, theologians, etc. There was not a uniform answer to their quest about what it is that truly gives meaning to life. The diverse nature of their views is largely due to their different backgrounds, schools of thought, orientations and future expectations. Beyond the persons making the inquiries into meaning, there is an additional problem – a linguistic one – which is associated with the word 'meaning' itself.

Among philosophers of language or linguists, there are several senses of the word 'meaning'. Scholars such as Max Black, Rudolf Carnap and William Alston discussed extensively the different nuances of meaning. Max Black maintains that the word 'meaning' is an ambiguous word that depicts at least four cardinal meanings: Intention or purpose, designation or reference, definition or translation and causal antecedent/consequences.[1]

While Rudolf Carnap gives a classification of the kinds of meaning in the field of semiotics as follows:

Cognitive (Theoretic/Assertive Meaning) – which arises when a sentence asserts something; hence what is involved is the question of truth and falsehood.

---

[1] Max Black, Philosopher.

Factual Meaning – This is a case where the truth-value of cognitive meaning rests on both a semantic apprehension of a sentence and on the truth-value of facts referred to therein. While **Logical/Formal Meaning** is displayed when the truth-value depends only on the terms occurring in the sentence: analysing, for example, the sentence into subject, verb, etc.

Expressive Meaning – deals with cases when a sentence expresses something of the state of the speaker and this may or may not have a cognitive meaning. This kind of meaning sometimes involves the use of picture, emotion and volition.[2]

From the foregoing, it is obvious that someone dealing with the subject matter of 'meaning' needs to explain the 'sense of meaning' that he/she is adopting. And whichever sense that one adopts would account for the way he/she would approach life.

Existential and Transcendental Considerations of Meaning

Perhaps, the best way to meditate existentially on the meaning of life is to ask oneself important questions. In other words, it is to pause and ponder, asking oneself occasionally the following questions: 'What is it that I consider meaningful for myself?' 'How would such meaning lead me to a lot of things?' 'In what do I really find meaning?' That is to say, 'what gives me real satisfaction and fulfilment?' Could it be the company of human persons or the possession of material goods like owning cars, houses, fat bank accounts? These existential questions are significant because the most sacred book, the bible, has forewarned us that, 'Where one's treasure is, there one's heart rests also' (cf. Mt 6:21).

The responses we give to the above questions will determine a lot about our attitude towards life, our plans for it, our approach towards

---

[2] Rudolf Carnap, Philosopher.

it and our reactions to its surprises. Generally, life with a good sense of meaning is preferable because it becomes a purpose-driven life.

Now, we all have the freedom and free will to determine what gives meaning to us. However, an important aspect of the question of meaning is: What is the yardstick with which we can 'weigh' and 'evaluate' the meaningfulness of an action/event or thing? If we wish to go for the excellent or perfect yardstick of meaningfulness of anything at all, then we must go beyond the human sphere, making a leap to the transcendental or divine sphere.

To consider the meaning transcendentally, we are confronted with such questions as these: Could that which satisfies and gratifies our egocentric needs be the real meaningful thing? Does 'meaningfulness' revolve around our temporal needs on earth alone without consideration of the divine plan? In other words, am I earthbound in my quest for meaning? Is my sense of meaning within the space-time region? These questions open us to an encompassing view that is holistic. Such a holistic view is better because man is not just a corporeal/material being, he is also a spiritual substance.

In determining our meaning in life, therefore, we must take into consideration the relevant aspects of the person – the body, the soul and the mind, etc. – everything that makes the human person. If all aspects of our being are properly noted then we may have a more balanced answer as to what constitutes meaning in life. This will enable us to know when one aspect of our lives is beginning to dominate the other or when one aspect is dictating the other.

Man, as a spiritual being, takes decisions not just based on the physical/material wellbeing of the person, but also of the spiritual wellbeing of the person. When we look deep into the well of the spiritual person, we discover a lot of meanings that go beyond all imaginable worldly benefits. We can understand that the meaning of life is far beyond this earthly sphere, which is short-lived, imperfect and non-eternal. A life that has a meaning is anchored on the transcendental or divine sphere, which is perfect, eternal and peaceful. It is a life governed by the spirit of God; a life that knows and acknowledges the author of life itself. It is the author of life who sent his Son, Jesus to be 'the Way, the Truth and the Life' (cf. Jn 14:6). When we dispose ourselves to follow this 'Way, Truth and Life', life automatically takes on new meaning for us. What constitutes the 'true meaning' of life is therefore not what we see, feel and touch, but the values that are beyond our world. It leads us to total abandonment of ourselves to the one who owns the world and the one we are engrafted to. He becomes the 'standard of meaningfulness' in our lives. *His meaning becomes 'my meaning'*. In him I experience 'true and real meaning' in life by allowing myself to be configured to him in such a manner that I see everything – good or bad situations – in the light of his Divine Providence.

Given this understanding, one sees the inappropriateness of the action of the purported Italian billionaire who took his life as we saw earlier. He failed to ask himself why God spared his own life and wealth – a light in a tunnel – that would have been employed to rekindle other lights for good. But since his 'standard of meaning' was narrowly set on his family members, once they were gone, he lost all motivation to live and took his own life. But when Jesus becomes the true meaning of one's life, i.e., when we discover and accept him as the owner of our personal lives, we find *real* meaning and proper orientation to life's events. However, when we do not find Jesus, we lose a deeper sense of meaning.

Conclusion

Our world today is broken, divided, unjust, uncharitable and lacking peace because the deeper meaning of life – a transcendental view – has eluded most of us. As soon as we can return to such a view, our world would be renewed to become a foretaste of that promised paradise, a wonderful place to be in. Discovering this meaning, we find peace even in the midst of many lacks: poverty, failure, disappointment and desolation. Thus, the main question of this reflection can now be answered: 'My meaning' is meaningful when anchored on the *transcendental/Divine* meaning, which is arrived at through holistic consideration and a patient discernment of Divine Illumination.

* * *

From the above reflections given by His Lordship to educate family members on how to attribute meaning to their lives, the questions that would probably confront the reader at this juncture might include the following:

- If all members of my household, including myself value our lives and really understand the meaning of being alive in the family, why are we not using every opportunity we have in the family to worship God in the comfort of our home, having known that he created us in his image and likeness?
- If life has meaning to all members of our household, why are some not ready to join us in our daily family devotion to make our domestic church livelier and more spirit-filled?
- If money is not more valuable than God to some people in my extended family, and also among some friends around me, why is it that on Sundays, they do not go to Church, and instead they open their stores in the market to continue with their daily struggles to make more and more money? The second part of this question is: When will such people ever have enough money in their account to stop and thank God for what they have already saved?
- Now that I personally know, after my deep reflections on my life, why God created me in his image and likeness, what changes do I make from this moment in my spiritual life to bring me closer and closer to our all-loving God?
- Now that I have reflected on the very reason why God sent me to this world through my family, what do I do from now on to

make my parents' lives much more spiritually oriented, worth living and dignified?

- Having been a member of the Holy Family Society, which promotes family devotion at home, what can I do from now on to get everyone in the family to become active participants in family devotion in a bid to strengthen our domestic church, with a view to making it quite welcoming to our immediate neighbour?

- Having learned a lot from this book and having had my own personal reflections on what I should hold dear in my life, what steps should I take now to follow the path of life that has been shown to me in this book, knowing full well that our Lord Jesus Christ is 'the Way, the Truth and the Life'?

- If I succeed in bringing some members of my family to the Church who do not yet know the meaning of life and are therefore wallowing in ignorance as they get themselves plunged deeper into secret cults, what steps do I take to get the Church to unbound them?

- Having reflected on the true meaning of life and what God has been directing my mind to, and which I have been rejecting for a long time because of my unholy, selfish desire to acquire illegal wealth and marry a wife or wives as the case may be, do I now firmly resolve from today to follow the path of life to go to the seminary (if still a young man) or go to a convent (if still a young girl) for the purpose of actualising God's will for me in becoming a reverend father or a reverend sister?

- Having fully reflected on the reasons why I am still in this world when many others born after me have been called back home, should I continue to be acquiring material things through fraudulent means in order to make my life comfortable in this world at the expense of losing the much more spiritually-comforting rooms in our Father's house in heaven, which our Lord Jesus Christ himself has gone before us to prepare in advance of our coming back to our real home if we do God's will here on earth?

These and many more questions should really agitate our minds after having deep reflections on the various topical and spiritual issues covered in this book.

May the almighty God grant us the wisdom to understand his messages being daily sent into our inner hearts, and may he prosper us spiritually as we take the bold steps to move on to the narrow road that will lead us successfully to his warm embrace when we finally arrive at our real home in heaven.

In conclusion, let us ask our merciful God to forgive us our sins for not attributing the correct meaning to his numerous calls on us individually, all this time, to follow the path of life that he himself directed us to take but which we have most likely abandoned for selfish reasons. We could then ask God that as we have now made a U-turn to answer his call, if he could please give us the opportunity to fulfil the purpose for which he created us. So, as this chapter comes to a close, let this be one of the spiritual messages to reflect on in order to have a positive change to our spiritual life if we are desirous of fulfilling the purpose of our existence in life.

7

Lessons About Life and Death: What to Teach in the Domestic Church

As earlier indicated in this book, the main purpose of founding the Holy Family Society is to return families to God, especially those whose members have derailed from the faith and have gone separate ways, thereby bringing about estrangement, disunity, lack of peace, trust and cohesion in the family. It is to help remedy this situation and prayerfully get everyone to journey together as a unique, indivisible family in the sight of God that the Holy Family Society exists.

It is also to use every available resource it has to get members and other Christians to work towards holiness all the time because no one knows when death will come. The question that the society wants all Christians and non-Christians to constantly reflect on is: 'When death comes, where will I go, heaven or hell?'. It is a question everyone must answer every day as we carry on with our daily activities and as we deal with our fellow human beings. This being the case, we need to make teaching about death a part of our curriculum in life. It is my view that the teaching should begin in the domestic church.

Teaching About Death

It is how to go about the teaching of death, which is certainly not such a popular subject or one that many people are willing to discuss, that is our focus in this chapter. The reason for this is that it is one of the main objectives of the Holy Family Society to get more and more people to strive daily towards holiness as they joyfully return themselves and their family members to God. It is this same desire that influences the design of its spiritual programmes. This invariably helps the society to create opportunities for more and more people to come into its fold, thereby experiencing tremendous growth. It is also important to re-emphasise here that in carrying out its programmes, the society has been relying heavily on spiritual support from the Catholic Church hierarchy for its spiritually inspired programmes.

Conscious of this support, the Holy Family Society designs its spiritual programmes in such a manner to use every available opportunity to evangelise and bring families back to God. Such opportunities come regularly as people celebrate birthdays, marriage anniversaries, promotions in the office, victories in elections, winning jackpots in lotteries, or receiving awards of chieftaincy titles as well as when couples celebrate their marriages or conduct the burial ceremonies of their loved ones.

Experience About Death

It has been our regular experience in the society that our members are invited from time to time to participate in the burial programmes of some active members. There came a time when our members participated in four burials within six weeks including that of one of our spiritual Fathers, Monsignor Patrick Usenbor who died on 4 February 2020, at the age of ninety-nine. It then dawned on me that all members of the Holy Family Society and indeed, all Christians should have a book to which they can refer, on how they are to prepare themselves for a holy death.

It is the result of my reflection on this subject that prompted the thoughts that are being expressed in this chapter. But before taking the reader into their thoughts on this subject, it is important that we stop a moment to pray especially for those who have returned to the

Lord from our family, from our society and from the Christian fold, etc., that the good Lord should have merciful judgement on each and every one of them (please observe one minute silence here). Eternal rest grant unto them O Lord. And let perpetual light shine upon them. May their souls and the souls of all the faithful departed, through the mercy of God rest in perfect peace.

There is no doubting the fact that by being present at burial programmes, we consciously or subconsciously learn good things, including the ones that usually strike most mourners deeply in their hearts, especially when it comes to the time to bid goodbye to the dead as his or her body is being lowered into the grave.

Reflections on Death

After attending burial ceremonies, it is instructive that we should return home to reflect on how we ourselves can achieve a holy death. It is to make this easier for our reflection as well as do so virtually every day that this book, particularly this chapter, is being introduced to the discerning public. Preparation for a holy death should be the concern of everyone, especially Christians because it makes no sense for Christians to go through this world as people who really worship God without getting to where Christ wants all Christians who have done the will of his Father here on earth to be. This, therefore, emphasises the importance of Christians taking it as an unavoidable duty to follow the guidelines that Christ himself has given to us in order to get to where he himself is, at our demise.

As earlier indicated, attending burial ceremonies should make us learn good things and reflect on issues that we cannot immediately find tangible answers to, but which we must place on our front burners every day. Such issues include:

(1) When will my own death come?
(2) Where will I die?
(3) How will my burial be?

(4) Who will officiate at my funeral Mass?

(5) Who will be present at my funeral ceremonies?

(6) How will my family thank God for the life he gave me on this earth?

(7) What will be awaiting me after members of my family have concluded their Thanksgiving Ceremonies and have gone home individually to continue with their own lives?

These are some of the questions that should always agitate our minds each time we come back from the funeral ceremonies of a spouse, a close family member, a friend, a reverend father or reverend sister. For us not to be completely lost in our thoughts on these issues, we need to begin to learn by ourselves as well as teach others in our domestic churches what the scriptures tell us about death and how to prepare for it.

In the scriptures, we learn about the Holy Family of Nazareth whom God graciously gave us as a model for imitation, to be able to live a good life in him. In imitating the Holy Family of Nazareth, God gave us a clear indication that we are going to go through a lot of suffering in life from our childhood, just as Jesus, tied to the back of Mother Mary and accompanied by her husband, Joseph, encountered many sufferings when they undertook a journey by night from Bethlehem to Egypt to avoid Jesus being killed in his infancy.

Herod, who was the king in Israel at that time 'had enquired from the priests the Christ who was to be born, and when they told him that this will be in Bethlehem of Judea; for so it is written by the prophet: "And you, O Bethlehem, in the land of Judea ... from you shall come a ruler who will govern my people Israel"' (Mt 2:4–6), so he began to execute a devilish plan on how to eliminate Jesus.

How Jesus Began His Suffering in Life

Herod, feeling that Jesus would be a threat to his kingship, quickly summoned three wise men instructing them as follows: 'Go and search diligently for the child and when you have found him bring me word that I too may go and worship him' (Mt 2:8).

But because of the deceitful words from King Herod, an angel of the Lord appeared to Joseph in a dream and said: 'Rise and take the child and his mother and flee to Egypt, and remain there till I tell you; for Herod is about to search for the child, to destroy him' (Mt 2:13).

The purpose of highlighting this story is to let the reader know that human beings can have enemies even from infancy and human sufferings can also begin from infancy just as Christ himself experienced. So, we need to stay right with God just as Joseph was, in order to have the angel of God directing our course in life. It is quite important for us to learn and teach our loved ones in our domestic churches that staying right with God does not prevent us from sufferings.

Sufferings Prepare One for Eternal Glory

In fact, the sufferings we encounter while carrying out our duties effectively and faithfully and/or while working in God's vineyard help greatly to prepare one for eternal glory as no one knows when death will knock at our door. This is what family members must learn from the domestic church, with perfect understanding that all our sufferings are to be united with that of Christ, which he himself experienced right from his birth and was concluded in his passion and death on the cross.

Family members must also learn how to use every occasion of suffering to atone for our sins and to thank God for preparing us for eternal glory. Suffering must be converted positively to a good end where we can joyfully look at the face of Christ smiling to us as he gives us more strength to continue the work that he has assigned to us. Neither the suffering we have encountered in working for our family or working for the Lord, nor the suffering we see ahead of us should discourage us from doing our work faithfully, no matter whose ox is gored.

All that we should keep in mind, which should always encourage us to bear our sufferings in a dignified manner is what St Paul told the Romans, when he said: 'I consider that the sufferings of this present time are not worth comparing with the glory that it is to be revealed to us. For the creation waits with eager longing for the revealing of the sons of God; for the creation was subjected to futility, not of its will but by the will of him who subjected it in hope, because the creation itself will be set free from its bondage to decay and obtain the glorious liberty of the children of God' (Rm 8:18–21).

Words of Joy Needed Daily From Our Hearts

If this occupies our thoughts when sufferings are unduly inflicted on us, what should come out of our mouths should be words of joy and not those of condemnation because we will certainly be set free at our demise and our Lord Jesus Christ himself will be there in heaven to receive us and grant us the glorious liberty of the children of God.

We should also learn from the short story about Joseph's flight to Egypt that apart from the suffering that Jesus, Mary and Joseph encountered on that trip, they found themselves in self-exile. This is an indication to us that we may also find it necessary sometimes to create some distance between us and our perceived enemy, without planning any evil against such a person or the institution that is working against us. We may even decide to go on our own self-exile if the forces of evil are determined to drag us down for no just cause. Such a decision can create time for the ill-wind to blow out before returning to do the work God has assigned to one, just as the Holy Family did.

It is for everyone to clearly understand from Christ's example that I have directed attention to the fact that certain sufferings are necessary for our safety in the world and for our salvation. To help us understand that every day is meant for us to prepare for death, our Lord Jesus Christ spent quality time teaching us the Beatitudes in Matthew 5:3–12, all in his effort to clarify everything that should attract our attention in life. He more or less summarised these as crucial elements that we must study and struggle to put into practice every day to help us prepare for a holy death, as death could come our way at any time.

8

Preparing for a Holy Death and Being With the Lord

From the previous chapter, we must have learnt that it is of utmost importance to prepare for a holy death because this is the most precious gift that we can give to ourselves. Let us imagine here that one buys the most expensive and beautiful house in the neighborhood for oneself. Even the rats, cockroaches, ants, lizards, moths, birds, as well as the human beings that are living with one will continue to live there if it happens that one's life is ended and one is going to the Great Beyond.

It is only then that many realise that the beautiful home and other properties left behind by the deceased cannot be taken along on the day the body is lowered into the grave. At such a moment one finds that whatever one had acquired in this world, be it houses, lands, companies, educational qualifications, political positions, etc., apart from one's good name, does not work to any advantage after death.

A Good Name Accompanies One Into the Grave

It is therefore of utmost importance that a good name to go along with us into our grave and to eternity must be worked for while we are still alive. And as we work very hard to earn a good name, we are, at the same time, preparing for a holy death. It is really not expensive to prepare for a holy death.

One does not even need to spend thousands of dollars to achieve this. The question that arises immediately from the inquisitive mind is: 'How can one have a holy death as one leaves this sinful world?'. This is a question that should be of immediate concern for everyone reading this book. To find the answer, Christ lovingly and generously presented to us the summary of his teaching on this subject, pointing out that:

> Blessed are the poor in spirit for theirs is the kingdom of heaven. Blessed are those who mourn, for they shall be comforted. Blessed are the meek for they shall inherit the earth. Blessed are those who hunger and thirst for righteousness, for they shall be satisfied. Blessed are the merciful, for they shall obtain mercy. Blessed are the pure in heart, for they shall see God. Blessed are the peacemakers, for they shall be called sons of God. Blessed are those who are persecuted for righteousness' sake, for theirs is the kingdom of heaven. Blessed are you when men revile you and persecute you and utter all kinds of evil against you falsely on my account. Rejoice and be glad, for your reward is great in heaven, for so men persecuted the prophets who were before you (Mt 5:3–12).

And just in case the criteria enumerated above for achieving a holy death are not easily understood by us, Christ went further to give us twenty-one guidelines as recorded in the Gospel of St Matthew on how we are to make the necessary sacrifices, possibly every day, to follow the righteous, narrow path already designed for us as we navigate this world. It is only then, he assures, that we will arrive at the narrow gate, after receiving a gracious gift of a holy death as a reward for the way in which one has managed his or her life in this world. So, a holy death is a precious gift that is not paid for, hence even the poorest persons on the planet are entitled to receive this spiritual gift.

Now, let us look at the twenty-one guidelines that can assist any person, whether rich or poor, to achieve a holy death.

Twenty-One Guidelines to Help Us Play Our Part Well in Life and Prepare for a Holy Death

As Christians study Christ's teachings in the bible, and as we listen to our ordained pastors in the Church, among those who are desirous of experiencing holy deaths in our families, many have come to realise that it is most important to effectively use our domestic church to educate members of our families on the twenty-one guidelines that Christ himself gave to enable us to navigate our path through life. These have become the surest ways for arriving at the narrow gate in spite of the difficulties and sufferings that may come our way. Jesus specially presented these to us to make us prepare for a holy death at any time.

To understand Christ's teachings and to learn how to incorporate them into our day-to-day living, the reader is hereby presented with the summary of the guidelines. These should make us live our lives to the fullest and return happily to the warm embrace of our Father in heaven after a holy death here on earth.

Let it be made clear that living one's life to the fullest does not mean living to a very old age. Living one's life to the fullest in my reasoning is when one has duly completed the assignments that God has generously given to one, and when there is a clear indication to the Father that one has faithfully done his will here on earth.

Confusion About Long Life for Evil Men

Sometimes people get confused about this when they see people who they consider evil live to a ripe old age and then they begin to wonder if God is really fair in giving such people a long time to live on earth. In fact, instead of thinking negatively about such a situation, we should get on our knees to thank God for his benevolence for giving such persons a long time to make amends to their individual lives. Those who make good use of the time given to them by God could be seen as the repentant sinners who, just like the 'repentant criminal' on the cross, tied side by side with Jesus Christ, who seized the opportunity at the eleventh hour to repent and plead with Christ to allow him, a sinner, to go with him to paradise. But before the repentant criminal confessed his sins, he was moved to rebuke his own colleague in criminal activities who had joined others to mock Christ, saying: 'Do you not fear God, since you are under the same sentence of condemnation? And we indeed justly; for we are receiving the due reward of our deeds; but this man has done nothing wrong' (Lk 23:40–41). After this confession, he wholeheartedly pleaded with Jesus, saying: 'Jesus, remember me when you come in your kingly power'. His request was granted as Jesus said: 'Truly, I say to you, today you will be with me in paradise' (Lk 23:42–43).

Making Atonement for Our Sins

Everyone, whether seen as good or evil, has a chance to make atonement for his or her sins. God can give any person a long time to do this during the course of their life and we cannot question his generosity for doing this. We should know that very many holy men also live to a ripe old age. What should concern us greatly here is that it behoves the individual whom God joyfully made in his image and likeness to, first and foremost, discern the purpose for which God sent them to this world. Thereafter, we should strive always to follow the crucial guidelines that Christ has given to us to help us fulfil that same purpose. And if we are not able to follow the guidelines, and as a result, commit grievous sins, we should understand that our benevolent God always gives us a long time to cover up our multitude of sins by the good works we do, and by our resolve to keep our faith in him. We should therefore not be shy to come daily or periodically to God, especially when we have sinned, to tell him we are sorry. This is what we can easily do when we confess our sins to an anointed priest of God. Our God is all-loving, and ready to forgive at any time as he loves us more than we even love ourselves.

Thirsting for God

It is quite instructive for us to know that we can only keep our faith in God by thirsting for him and making ourselves available for confession from time to time. These acts, as simple as they are, help us greatly to live our lives to the fullest.

Let it also be understood here that faith without good works is dead. St James teaches us thus: 'What does it profit, my brethren, if a man says he has faith but has not works? Can his faith save him? If a brother or sister is poorly clothed and in lack of daily food, and one of you says to them, "Go in peace, be warmed and filled" without giving the things needed for the body, what does it profit? So, faith by itself, if it has no works, is dead' (Jas 2:14–17).

Meanwhile, let us look at the crucial guidelines that Christ gave us to enable us to live our lives to the fullest and prepare for a holy death. They are as follows:

(1) That we are to be salt and light; as salt, we must provide nutrients for the earth to produce good fruits; and as light of the world, we must let our 'light so shine before men, that they may see our good works and give glory to our Father who is in heaven' (Mt 5:16).

(2) That it was said to men of old: '"You shall not kill; and whoever kills shall be liable to judgement." But I say to you whoever is angry with his brother shall be liable to judgement; whoever insults his brother shall be liable to the council and whoever says, "you fool" shall be liable to hell fire. So, if you are offering your gift at the altar; and remember that your brother has something against you, leave your gift before the altar and go; first to be reconciled with your brother and then come and offer your gift. Make friends quickly with your accuser, while you are going with him to court' (Mt 5:21–25).

(3) That it was said to men of old: '"You shall not commit adultery." But I say to you that everyone who looks at a woman

lustfully has already committed adultery with her in his heart. If your right eye causes you to sin, pluck it out and throw it away; it is better that you lose one of your members than your whole body be thrown into hell' (Mt 5:27–30).

(4) That it was said to men of old: '"Whoever divorces his wife, let him give her a certificate of divorce". But I say to you that everyone who divorces his wife, except on the ground of unchastity, makes her an adulteress and whoever marries a divorced woman commits adultery' (Mt 5:31–32).

(5) That it was said to men of old: '"You shall not swear falsely, but shall perform to the Lord what you have sworn." But I say to you, "Do not swear at all, either by heaven, for it is the throne of God, or by the earth, for it is his footstool or by Jerusalem, for it is the city of the great King"' (Mt 5:33–35).

(6) That it was said to men of old: '"An eye for an eye and a tooth for a tooth." But I say to you, "Do not resist one who is evil. But if anyone strikes you on the right cheek, turn to him the other also"' (Mt 5:38–39).

(7) That it was said to men of old: '"You shall love your neighbour and hate your enemy." But I say to you, love your enemies and pray for those who persecute you, so that you may be sons of your Father who is in heaven; for he makes sun rise on the evil and on the good, and sends rain on the just and on the unjust ... You therefore, must be perfect, as your heavenly Father is perfect' (Mt 5:43–48).

(8) That: 'When you give alms, sound no trumpet before you, as the hypocrites do, in the synagogues and in the streets, that they may be praised by men. Truly, I say to you, they have their reward. But when you give alms, do not let your left hand know what your right hand is doing, so that your alms may be in secret; and your Father who sees in secret will reward you' (Mt 6:2–4).

(9) That when it comes to prayer, which we are encouraged to say regularly, we should understand that: 'When you pray, you must not be like the hypocrites, for they love to stand and pray in the synagogues and in the street corners, that they may be seen by men. Truly, I say to you, they have their reward. But when you pray, go into your room and shut the door and pray to your Father who is in secret; and your Father who sees in secret will reward you' (Mt 6:5–6).

(10) That for us to understand the type of fasting that is acceptable to God, we should take note that: 'When you fast, do not look dismal, like the hypocrites, for they disfigure their faces that their fasting may be known by men. Truly, I say to you, they had their reward. But when you fast, anoint your head and wash your face, that your fasting may not be seen by men but by your Father who is in secret; and your Father who sees in secret will reward you' (Mt 6:16–18).

(11) That on the issue of material wealth, which many unnecessarily fight over for, and for which some people are even ready to kill other human beings, Christ warns: 'Do not lay for yourselves treasures on earth, where moth and rust consume and where thieves break in and steal, but lay up for yourselves treasures in heaven, where neither moth nor rust consumes and where thieves do not break in and steal. For where your treasure is, there will your heart be also' (Mt 6:19–21).

(12) That for us to always avoid shady deals and evil acts, whether done in darkness or during daylight, Christ says: 'The eye is the lamp of the body. So, if your eye is sound, your whole body will be full of light; but if your eye is not sound, your whole body will be full of darkness. If then the light in you is darkness, how great is that darkness!' (Mt 6:22–23).

(13) To warn us about being in a club of evildoers or worshipping idols that come in different forms, Christ makes

it clear to us that: 'No one can serve two masters, for either he will hate the one and love the other, or he will be devoted to the one and despise the other. You cannot serve God and mammon' (Mt 6:24).

(14) To keep us away from craving for things we do not have instead of using the time to thank God for what we do have, including our own lives, Christ instructs thus: 'Do not be anxious about your life, what you shall eat or what you shall drink, nor about your body, what you shall put on. Is not life more than food, and the body more than clothing? Look at the birds of the air; they neither sow nor reap nor gather into barns and yet your heavenly Father feeds them. Are you not of more value than they?' (Mt 6:25–26).

(15) Because we are often quick in finding faults with others, Christ also warns: 'Judge not, that you be not judged. For with the judgement you pronounce you will be judged, and the measure you give will be the measure you get' (Mt 7:1–2).

(16) On being very careful with the evil person, Christ advises: 'Do not give dogs what is holy; and do not throw your pearls before swine, lest they trample them underfoot and turn to attack you' (Mt 7:6).

(17) For us not to remain complacent or ignore reaching out to God, Christ reminds us of the need to thirst always for God, pointing out that it is only when you *ask* that it will be given to you: 'seek and you will find; knock and it will be opened to you. For everyone who asks receives, and he who seeks, finds, and to him who knocks it will be opened' (Mt 7:7–8).

(18) And to ensure that all our struggles in life are directed toward winning eternal life, Christ encourages us to strive to enter by 'the narrow gate; for the gate is wide and the way is easy, that leads to destruction, and those who enter by it are

many. For the gate is narrow and the way is hard, that leads to life, and those who find it are few' (Mt 7:13–14).

(19) Knowing that some people may be tempted to follow false prophets, as in the case of the Maitama woman in the true-life story related in Volume One, Chapter One (from p. 55), Christ strongly warns us: 'Beware of false prophets, who come to you in sheep's clothing. You will know them by their fruits … A sound tree cannot bear evil fruit, nor can a bad tree bear good fruit' (Mt 7:15–18).

(20) Emphasising the importance of doing God's will on earth, Christ reveals that: 'Not everyone who says to me, "Lord, Lord" will enter the kingdom of heaven, but he who does the will of my father who is in heaven' (Mt 7:21).

(21) And for us to be on the side of the wise men who follow God's law, and to encourage all of us to be hearers and doers of God's word, Christ reveals to us that: 'Everyone then who hears these words of mine and does them will be like a wise man who built his house upon a rock, and the rain fell, and the floods came, and the winds blew and beat upon that house, but it did not fall, because it has been founded on a rock. And everyone who hears these words of mine and does not do them will be like a foolish man who builds his house upon the sand; and the rain fell, and the flood came, and the winds blew and beat against that house, and it fell; and great was the fall of it' (Mt 7:24–27).

If we diligently follow the twenty-one guidelines above and obey God's commandments, nothing will pull us down from the ladder of holiness and we will not experience any form of regret in our decision to move only towards God's embrace whenever our time is up here on earth. As God himself is aware that we can easily cross the red line here on earth if we look elsewhere and, in the process ignore any of the guidelines and/or disobey his commandments, he will still not abandon us if we quickly come back to him in supplication, begging for mercy and help. This is because the Psalmist has assured us that: 'The Lord is merciful and gracious, slow to anger and abounding in mercy. He will not always chide nor will he keep his anger forever. He does not deal with us according to our sins, nor repay us according to our iniquities. For as the heavens are high above the earth, so great is his mercy toward those who fear him' (Ps 103:8–11).

So, all that we need to do is to keep striving to follow the guidelines and obey God's commandments. God himself assured us that: 'Whoever obeys me will not be put to shame, and those who work with my help will not sin' (Sir 24:22).

Having known this, it behoves each and every one of us to always seek the help of God to enable us to follow his guidelines creditably as well as obey his commandments. This is necessary because by ourselves we cannot do much without crossing the red line. So, every day, we must be on our knees calling for God's help, knowing full well that as we do our daily duties, interact with one another, strive to meet our responsibilities to our family, to our neighbour, and to our Church, we may cross the red line. This explains why, in spite of our struggles to keep our domestic church functional, we need to stay close to the priest in order to confess our sins from time to time, attend Holy Mass on daily basis, if it is possible to do so, and re-energise ourselves constantly with the reception of the Holy Eucharist.

Individual Cases on the Day of Judgement
If the above guidelines give us a clear exposition on how to conduct our individual lives here on earth, we should also take note that every day, Christ places on our table another exposition on how he will handle our individual cases on the Day of Judgement. He reveals that:

> When the Son of Man comes in his glory, and all the angels with him, then he will sit on his glorious throne. Before him

will be gathered all the nations, and he will separate them one from another as a shepherd separates the sheep from the goats and he will place the sheep at his right and the goats at his left. Then the King will say to those at his right hand, 'Come O blessed of my Father, inherit the kingdom prepared for you from the foundation of the world; for I was hungry and you gave me food, I was thirsty and you gave me drink, I was a stranger, and you welcome me. I was naked, you clothed me, I was sick, and you visited me, I was in prison, and you came to see me.' Then the righteous will answer him, 'Lord when did we see you hungry and feed you or thirsty and give you drink? And when did we see you a stranger and welcome you, or naked and clothe you? And when did we see you sick or in prison and visit you?' And the King will answer them 'Truly, I say to you as you did it to one of the least of these my brethren, you did it to me'. Then, he will say to those at his left hand, 'Depart from me you accursed into the eternal fire prepared for the devil and his angels, for I was hungry and you gave me no food, and I was thirsty and you gave no drink' ... And they will go away into eternal punishment, but the righteous into eternal life (Mt 25:31–46).

As we have been privileged as Christians to receive these expositions from Jesus Christ himself, on what we need to do in our daily living to win eternal life, and how we are to be judged on the Day of Judgement, it is therefore left to us to do whatever is humanly possible to strive always to achieve holiness from the way we conduct our daily lives.

Seven Steps of Holiness

For us to achieve a state of holiness, the Fathers of the Church have pointed out, in so many ways, that holiness consists of seven main steps. These steps were again re-emphasised by Rev. Fr Joseph Mary

Wolfe, MFVA, in his homily during a Mass he celebrated and relayed through the Eternal World Television Network (EWTN).

The reader may want to know that Rev. Fr Joseph Mary, as he is popularly known, is one of the priests of the Order of the Franciscan Missionaries of the Eternal Word, known in Latin as *Missionarii Franciscani Verbi Aeterni* (MFVA). He was an electrical engineer who was attracted to the priesthood while working for Mother Angelica at EWTN. In the homily referred to above, he listed the seven steps that constitute holiness as follows:

(1) Having a childlike attitude towards things

(2) Having a strong love for the Eucharist

(3) Having a faithful devotion to the Blessed Mother of God

(4) Doing ordinary things in life in an extraordinary manner by giving attention to detail

(5) Embracing the sufferings that come our way and linking such sufferings with the sufferings of our Lord, Jesus Christ

(6) Having a holy desire to please God by ensuring that we have filial love for him and doing things in the best interest of others

(7) Creating a sense of humour in a genuine desire to bring joy to others

Fr Joseph Mary Wolfe, MFVA noted that if we apply this set of principles to our daily life, we will begin to see a remarkable difference in our efforts towards holiness.[1]

---

[1] Fr Joseph Mary Wolfe, EWTN Homily (these seven steps can also be found online: Rev. Peter M.J. Stravinskas, *Catholic World Report*, "'All the way to Heaven is Heaven": 7 basic steps to holiness', https://www.catholicworldreport.com/2017/11/29/all-the-way-to-heaven-is-heaven-7-basic-steps-to-holiness/; accessed on 23 November 2021).

As God has generously given each and every one of us our individual life to live, and as Christ himself has also given us guidelines on how to live our life to the fullest, our struggle in life should therefore be aimed towards achieving a state of holiness in order to prepare for a holy death at any time. In doing so, the seven steps that constitute holiness, which Fr Joseph Mary Wolfe, MFVA of EWTN, referred to in his homily should be put into practice as these are meant to help us work towards perfection, and keep us ready for holy death.

Evil Forces in the World
From what has been reflected on so far in this chapter, there is the need to re-emphasise here that good practising Christians should always adopt and exhibit good Christian attitudes at home and in public. This is because there are many evil forces around us almost everywhere in the world. We often find that, 'we are afflicted in every way, but not crushed; perplexed but not driven to despair; persecuted but not forsaken; struck down but not destroyed; always carrying in our bodies the death of Jesus, so that the life of Jesus may also be manifested in our bodies. For while we live, we are always being given up to death for Jesus' sake, so that the life of Jesus may be manifested in our mortal flesh' (2 Cor 4:8–11). These words of consolation and encouragement should be flowing in our hearts from time to time.

Before we look at other aspects of preparation for a holy death, we also need to emphasise that if parents, grandparents and other elders teach on the subject of holy death regularly in the domestic church, there will be much more sanity in the world. One will undoubtedly find that there will be less unruly behaviour and criminal activity in our communities. There will also be greater assurance that more and more people will be unavoidably focused on striving towards holiness during their earthly journey.

People will have the hope 'that we who are alive, who are left until the coming of the Lord, shall not precede those who have fallen asleep. For the Lord himself will descend from heaven with a cry of command, with the archangel's call, and with the sound of the trumpet of God. And the dead in Christ will rise first, then we who are alive, who are left, shall be caught up together with them in the clouds to meet the Lord in the air; and so we shall always be with the Lord' (1 Th 4:15–17).

This message from St Paul to the Thessalonians and also to ourselves should encourage all Christians to keep clinging to the Lord so that on the last day when the trumpet blows all of us will assemble before him in heaven as members of the same family. It is my prayer that Christian and non-Christian families alike will instructively undergo spiritual purifications before the 'D-Day' so that all will be there to answer their individual names before the Lord.

Spiritual Purification and Five Other Steps to Aid Holy Death

The spiritual purification that everyone needs to undergo should culminate with the confession of our sins. If we do have some difficulty in physically getting to the anointed priest of God to confess our sins, let us make some efforts to invite him to where he can reach us, either in the hospital or in the place we currently live. But if all efforts fail, then we should cultivate the holy desire to confess our sins. As we make strenuous efforts to reconcile ourselves with God, we should also take steps to do the following while preparing for a holy death:

(1) Clearing one's outstanding debts: If one has the means to clear one's outstanding debts, one should not procrastinate over it. One is to ensure that he or she gives the necessary directives to his or her immediate family members or trusted family friends that can act on one's behalf. It has always proved better to rely on one's spouse or own biological son or daughter to carry out one's instructions while on the deathbed or after one's demise. Since no one can predict when death will knock at the

door, it is advisable that the necessary instructions are given in advance when one is still sound and alert. Such instructions could culminate in a Will prepared by oneself witnessed by a legal practitioner and registered in the Registry of a High Court.

(2) Detaching oneself from material possessions: it is only when one is still alive that one can detach oneself from material possessions. No one needs to emphasise this to us because we came into this world naked and empty handed, and we are going to return to our God in the same way. It is therefore to our benefit and honour to detach ourselves of all material possessions before we exit this world. Parents who have items they have not used in the last two years and may not need in the next three years will need to share them with their loved ones and with the poor in society. The things that one could see as justified to keep are those that yield monthly or annual income to feed the family, ensure mobility and attend to welfare and medical needs. Once these are assured, then other material items, including landed properties of which the sale or yearly/monthly income will not add to one's comfort or improve one's family spirituality, should be shared to members of the family and those in greatest need. To avoid any ambiguity in this matter, there is the need to incorporate one's instructions in a Will to be written by oneself, endorsed by a lawyer and registered in the Registry of a High Court.

(3) Gifts to the Church, charitable organisations and persons outside the immediate family. Such gifts that one has decided to present to such bodies are better given when one is still alive than to wait for others to do this on one's behalf. The reason is that one can never be sure that people will do them in the way one would have loved to see them done in an orderly manner. So, without waiting until one gets sick or until one can no longer attend to relevant matters concerning one. It is advisable

that material gifts that are going to institutions and/or persons outside the family are quickly identified and shared out before one's death. And to avoid confrontations and unnecessary disputes in the future, what has been given out, and to whom they were given, should also be documented and incorporated in the Will.

(4) Material items that bring an income. Before one's death, the items that bring an income to sustain the family must be listed well in advance and noted as to whom they will be shared among the immediate members of one's family. In a situation where many properties are involved, one or two properties could be reserved as 'family property' that should be in the name of the surviving children that will continue to yield income for all members of the immediate family. This is to be seen as a source of promoting unity and togetherness in the family. The named family property and the reason for its being so named should be well spelt out in the Will that is prepared by one, endorsed by a legal practitioner and registered in the Registry of a High Court.

(5) Family projects, companies, organisations and programmes that would be left behind. One has a responsibility to list out projects, companies, organisations and programmes that one is desirous to entrust to family members who will see to their continuity after one's exit from the world. Immediate family members should be named as responsible for their continuity. To this end, they are to be given all the necessary documents and access to the remaining funds and other properties for their administration and continuity. They are also to use their talent, time, treasure and energy to ensure that such projects, companies, organisations and programmes are not discontinued. All these are also to be crafted into the Will that will be left behind for the children.

Disclosing the Administrators of One's Estate

Before one's exit, the children should be introduced to these projects, companies, organisations and programmes so that they become active participants when one is still alive. One's Will should also be disclosed to members of one's biological family before one's demise. But those who are not inclined to do this should then let them know who the administrators of the estate will be after the registered Will has been retrieved from the court.

If one takes immediate initiatives to go along with meeting one's commitments, with a view to organising one's life in the way suggested above, one will find that they have taken reasonable steps to prepare for a holy death. This is what I would want all members of my family, all members of the Holy Family Society, all Christians and non-Christians alike to put into practice.

In doing so, all of us should remember the highly treasured virtues of Jesus, Mary and Joseph, the Holy Family of Nazareth. To emulate them is to put into practice their virtues of humility, simplicity, obedience, prayerfulness, patience, self-abandonment, hard work, agape love, faithfulness, loving kindness, etc.

To get people to respond positively to this, with a view to having those who do the will of the Father in heaven being received into the warm embrace of the Lord at the time of our exit from this world, is the reason for the existence of the Holy Family Society. May the good Lord continue to prosper all its members and all those who support its work in our community. And may the almighty God continue also to equip this society spiritually to enable us to execute its programmes successfully in the new evangelisation mission.

9

When Death Knocks at the Door

As earlier indicated in Chapter Seven and re-emphasised in Chapter Eight above, no matter which way we live our life in this world, death will knock at our door one day. No one knows when this will be. It could be today, tomorrow, next week, next month, next year, in five years' time, in ten years' time, twenty years' time; thirty years' time or at any time.

The bottom line is that no one knows when he or she will breathe his or her last in this world. This explains why I have specially dedicated Chapter Eight to my reflection on holy death.

The reader may want to know that as I was concluding work on this book, the invisible train of death struck my very dear cousin, Chief Edwin Eduwuirofo Ekhator, the Obasogie of Benin Kingdom, causing him to stretch and collapse while eating with his wife at the table.

As the wife could not imagine what was happening to her husband, she immediately called for help and all who came joined her in putting him into a vehicle to be rushed to the nearest hospital. On their arrival there, the doctors examined him and advised that he should be taken to the University of Benin Teaching Hospital (UBTH), where they have better facilities at the Intensive Care Unit (ICU). The wife and many of my relations then rushed him, without any waste of time to UBTH, where very experienced doctors examined him again and declared him dead on arrival.

In the confusion that followed amidst sobbing by family members at the hospital, the family decided there and then that his body should not be left in the hospital but would be taken home to see if he could come out of his suspected 'deep coma'. The family at this point could not rely on the declaration of the doctors at UBTH. It was after keeping vigil with him for twenty-four hours that it dawned on everyone that what the doctors at UBTH had said was true.

The core message to everyone here is that death can really come like a thief without giving any notice to the one to be robbed. Death comes at a time when one least expects such a thing to happen, hence the need to prepare for a holy death as indicated in Chapter Eight above.

Another point of this personal reflection that I shared with my family members as they were all mourning the passing away of my cousin, Chief Edwin Eduwuirofo Ekhator, had to do with the importance of praying for the dead. I took some time after the burial to share my thoughts on this very important topic to all mourners in the family; to visitors who came to deliver their messages of condolence, and to those who forwarded theirs to my phone. The reader may also want to share the message I sent out to many a day after my cousin's burial.

Titled, 'The Way to God is Wide Open for Everyone' this reflection was meant to highlight, and also explain, what I strongly feel about death. It was proposed as a message that people can always reflect on at a time of mourning the death of a family member, a friend, a close associate or even an enemy. I pointed out that from the experience of the sudden death of Chief Edwin Eduwuirofo Ekhator, everyone should take some time now to reflect on three important questions:

(1) What does death really mean to me?

(2) What should be one's last wishes, when death comes knocking unexpectedly at one's door, that a person wants his or her family members and others to respect?

(3) What do I, as an individual, consider as the most important thing to do for the dead before and after his or her burial?

I indicated in this message to the mourners that while people can be left on their own to reflect on the first two questions and give their individual answers, I would concern myself with making my personal views on the third question known, and other matters about death, generally. Below is the reflection I sent out advising what is best for mourners to do for my cousin:

My own personal view, without mincing words, is simply praying sincerely for the repose of the soul of the departed.

Many do this because they know that our God is a merciful Father who is ready to forgive us our sins when we devotedly request him to be merciful in judging us, especially on the last day. The dead, who can no longer do this are blessed to have people do it on their behalf.

Let it be known that there is no coercion involved and no imposition on anyone as to what type of prayers to say for the dead. Unfortunately, people sometimes misunderstand the intentions of those who come out boldly to pray for the dead. It should be understood that praying for the dead is the best gift we can give to them.

It is not the number of cows we buy to see that people attending burial ceremonies go home with chunks of meat. It is also not the number of musical bands that are hired to perform.

What then is important for the dead? The answer is prayer! prayer!! prayer!!!

It should also be clear to all that the period of mourning of the bereaved and other sympathisers usually brings out the best time for reflections – reflecting on the life and times of the dead and also reflecting on one's own life.

This is why the Lenten period provides ample opportunities for people to make genuine reflections about their personal lives, and thereafter come to terms about what to do to make amendments to their lifestyles, with a view to coming closer to God.

What many face while mourning the dead of a loved one in good faith is not quite different from what many go through when reflecting on the sufferings, passion, crucifixion, death and burial of our Lord Jesus Christ.

Let it be clear here that the situations people face while mourning the death of a loved one include:

(1) Experiencing pains that go directly to one's bone marrow. There is no doubt about receiving such pains also in the heart but one soon realises that there is nothing one can do about it. Another question that also agitates the genuine mourner's mind is: How can I then help the dead through prayers to gain heaven? This is the essence of having family members, friends and well-wishers who can help to organise continuous, soul-elevating prayers for the dead.

An example is the fourteen days of continuous prayers that my own family members organised for our parents who died separately in 1997 (my father who clocked 121 years), and in 2001 (my mother who exited at the age of 96), before they were laid to rest. Other activities, which featured prayer sessions for them, did not stop immediately after their burial ceremonies.

No one was forced to come daily or every week to participate in the prayers, but those who honoured the invitations benefited spiritually. It is on record that some were converted during the period.

(2) A personal, genuine reflection on death can go a long way not only to bring about conversion of hearts but also to bring about discernment, knowing what God has sent one to do in this life and how to go about it.

So, bereavement, as painful as it is, creates room for many good things to also happen in the family, in the community and in the world at large.

Unless the grain dies, one cannot see the good fruits that will emerge thereafter. Our Lord Jesus Christ made this very clear to us when he said: 'Truly, truly, I say to you, unless a grain of wheat falls into the earth and dies, it remains alone; but if it dies, it bears much fruit' (Jn 12:24).

This gives great hope for the coming generations. We must also remember that Christ himself died for all of us to atone for our sins and to show us the way to our Father in heaven.

So, the arrangements that are made for the Thanksgiving Mass and other prayers that are said during burial ceremonies are meant to help everyone in the family, and in the community as well as other participants to be focused on the gains of helping the dead to find the narrow road to heaven as the participants themselves gain a better understanding of what to do in life to make it to heaven.

Many may take the message seriously and profit from it and many more could reject it.

This is my personal message for reflection as we attend funeral ceremonies. Others can also share their own thoughts on this grave issue for many to benefit from.

May the good Lord rain his choicest blessings on all who are participating in different ways to peacefully lead my late cousin, Chief Edwin Eduwuirofo Ekhator to his final home.

Eternal rest grant unto him O Lord. And let perpetual light shine upon him!

May his soul and the souls of all the faithful departed through the mercy of God rest in perfect peace.

With God, all things are possible!

To Him alone be all glory and honour;

So that by his special Grace, heaven is our home!!!

Sir David E. Osunde
Founder/National Coordinator
Holy Family Society

As the reader reflects on the message above, the aspects I really want to emphasise at this point are three-fold. They are:

(1) The need to take a second look at the title of the reflection above: 'The Way to God is Wide Open for Everyone'

(2) The necessity for continuous prayers for the repose of the soul of the deceased after burial ceremonies

(3) The need for a passionate plea by genuine mourners for God's forgiveness of the sins the deceased committed while here on earth

Pope Francis in his new encyclical dated 3 October 2020, titled *Fratteli Tutti*, rightfully presented an interesting perspective about the human being in Paragraph 213 when he pointed out: 'That every human being possesses an inalienable dignity is a truth that corresponds to human nature apart from all cultural change. For this reason, human beings have the same inviolable dignity in every age of history and no one can consider himself or herself authorised by particular situations to deny this conviction or act against it'.[1] It is to respect the 'inalienable dignity' of the dead that what is considered

---

[1] Pope Francis, Encyclical Letter *Fratelli Tutti*, Vatican, 2020.

best should be given to them. From the perspective of the Catholic Church, this is undoubtedly the gift of offering Holy Mass for the dead.

Having taken note of this, it is also worth the while to understand here that the title of this reflection, 'The Way to God is Wide Open for Everyone', was graciously crafted for the reader to reflect on, and possibly understand, that in the world, there are many religions that have millions of followers as their adherents. There are also millions of people who refuse to follow the teachings of the known religions and want to be seen as non-conformists or atheists. Most of those who follow the different religions believe that the way they practice their own religion will lead them to God, probably because we all come from God, and God is everywhere, watching everyone.

But what many have failed to acknowledge is that heaven and hell are not seen by the human eyes from the world. Everyone should know that there are two different roads, which can only be reached by individuals as they exit from different places at different times from this world. What lead people to any of the two roads are what we have in our record of activities during our short or long stay on this earth. The scriptures clearly reveal to us all what the two different roads look like: while the one to heaven is narrow and bumpy, and many do not want to take it, the road to hell is wide and quite comfortable and many rush to take it.

It should be noted here that individuals use their own legs, as it were, to walk their way either to heaven or to hell, depending on the individual record of activities that each person holds tightly to his or her chest regarding how one has spent their time here on earth. No one can blame another for the choices people make by themselves in this respect, except perhaps in situations where some people are known to have been forced by others, especially by parents or friends, to take the wide route against their own will. Such persons who deceive others will also have to account for their nefarious actions.

From all indications, there are many out there in different parts of the world who are definitely confused about which route to really take. The scripture advises such persons thus: 'Enter by the narrow gate; for the gate is wide and the way is easy, that leads to destruction, and those who enter by it are many. For the gate is narrow and the way is hard, that leads to life, and those who take it are few' (Mt 7:13–14).

Everyone who reads and understand this scriptural message is expected to decide on his or her own which way to go. The same scripture makes it clear that God 'created man in the beginning and he left him in the power of his own inclination' (Sir 15:14). So, our God has generously given everyone the 'power' and the free will to live his or her life the way he or she wants in this world. For us to not miss our way to heaven, he generously gave us the example of Jesus, Mary and Joseph, the Holy Family of Nazareth, who lived their lives in this same world before returning to him. Everyone is therefore urged to imitate them. But those who do not want to follow their example also have the free will to go according to their 'own inclination'.

Praying for the Forgiveness of Sins of the Deceased

It is very important for everyone to realise that as human beings, we are not perfect. The result is that our shortcomings build up from day to day. This happens because we fall short of really understanding and fully obeying the Ten Commandments that God has given to us. And before we can claim to be perfect in obeying his commandments to the letter, one will need to be transformed first to become an angel of God and thereafter one can boastfully say he or she is free from sin in the world.

Historical records show that many of those who have been canonised as saints from time immemorial were sinners, but worked hard individually on their own to transform themselves to become holy people before they exited this world. The records that such people leave behind speak volumes about their holy encounters with people, and the spiritually fulfilling activities they were involved in during the various stages of their lives here on earth.

So, it is very rare, if not impossible, to find any human being in the world whose records will show that he or she never committed any sin. This is to say that, as human beings who have lived above the age of reasoning, there is no way any of us can live without committing sins against God and our neighbour.

It therefore behoves the sinner who fears God to find the properly established route through which he or she can seek forgiveness for their sins. If he or she cannot find such a route by themself, they should either be courageous enough to seek assistance from people regarding the steps to take before going to a priest for confession, or ignore completely the move towards reconciliation with God at his or her peril.

The sinner who does not bother about the number of sins he or she commits daily and possibly decides to increase his or her own tempo of committing sins, should not expect to go scot-free, for there is a price to pay individually for our sinful acts, just as we receive both spiritual and material rewards for our good deeds.

No one can stop the sinner from committing more and more sins. All that we need to know is that our merciful God is unarguably waiting for everyone on the Day of Judgement. Those who are wise don't need to wait until the last day before thinking of reconciling themselves with God and their neighbour. Our merciful God stretches his welcoming hands towards us every day as he gives us more time to leave our sinful ways in order to come to his warming embrace.

All we should know is that our sins against God and humanity cannot be covered up, hence the need for urgent reconciliation when we are still alive, knowing very well that: 'Nothing is covered up that will not be revealed, or hidden that will not be made known' (Lk 12:2). And if the sinner has no fear in their heart in committing grievous sins, let them know that the scripture adequately warns us to 'fear him who, after he has killed, has power to cast into hell, yes I tell you fear him!' (Lk 12:5).

So, no matter how holy we may assume we are as human beings, we must fear God and take adequate measures to atone for our sins when we are still alive. If we cannot do this before we die, the only option left is for our family members, friends and sympathisers to be on their knees on behalf of the deceased to plead with God to forgive the venial sins the deceased has committed against him and humanity.

It is therefore not out of place to state here that if the sinner knows, for instance, that death will knock on his or her door the next day, they will most certainly do everything possible to reconcile themself with God, and with their neighbour. There is no sane person in this world who knows the difference between heaven and hell that would willingly prefer to go to hell. So, for us and our loved ones to avoid going to hell, we all need to make supreme sacrifices to prepare for heaven, especially as no one knows when the bell is going to be rung. This explains why the scripture warns us in advance: 'But of that day and hour no one knows, not even the angels of heaven nor the Son of Man, but the Father alone' (Mt 24:36).

Since the Son of Man, our Lord Jesus Christ, was purposely sent to this world to show us the way to the Father's heart and kingdom, all that we are required to do is to listen to him. One important message he left with us is to use the structure he established for us in the world to win salvation for our souls. From the scriptures, people should know that when Jesus made Peter the rock on which he built his Church, he did not mince words when he told him: 'Truly, I say to you, whatever you bind on earth shall be bound in heaven, and whatever you loose on earth shall be loosed in heaven' (Mt 18:18).

This same mandate given to Peter to forgive sins, has through the power of anointment been given to succeeding popes as well as to validly ordained bishops and priests from time immemorial. With the presence of priests in our midst, many now have the opportunity to go to confessions for the forgiveness of their sins. And those who make good use of this opportunity always experience inner peace of mind and body, which gives a clear indication of their reconciliation with God.

Although this is known to be the established route for practising Catholics, and is well appreciated by them as a God-given gift for the cancellation of sins and reconciliation with him, those who are not Catholics are not condemned for not going through this spiritual route to reach the welcoming hands of God.

What Catholics believe they owe to such persons is to spend quality time praying for them from time to time whether they are alive or dead. One should not then be surprised to see that the Catholic Church and her followers emphasise the importance of fervent prayers for the dead more than the issue of refreshments for sympathisers and other participants at burial ceremonies. The Office of the Dead, specially meant to be used at the Wake-keep, is kept handy, to be used if the funeral programme makes allowance for it.

The issue of authentic prayer being said by the living for the dead is not a trivial matter in the Catholic Church. It is not something to be denied the dead, as this is the only way we can commune with God on their behalf. St Luke emphasises the importance of remaining persistent in presenting our intentions to God as we commune with him through prayer. This is the essence of his telling us the parable of the widow and the Unrighteous Judge in Luke 18:1–8, to buttress the fact that because of the persistence of the widow in her demand, the Unrighteous Judge had no option than to say: "'Though I neither fear God nor regard man, yet, because this widow bothers me, I will vindicate her, or she will wear me out by her continual coming." And the Lord said, "Hear what the Unrighteous Judge says. And will not God vindicate his elect, who cry to him day and night? Will he delay long over them? I tell you, he will vindicate them speedily'".

This should encourage all of us to constantly seek the face of God by being on our knees every day, making our intentions known to him through fervent prayer either for the living or for the dead. All we need to know is that it is not impossible for God to forgive the sins of those who, by our human judgement, are the worst sinners in our midst. Is there any wonder therefore that a priest has an obligation to say the highest form of prayer, which is the holy Mass, for both the living and the dead every day, week, month, and year, except of course if his faculty is suspended or he is impaired by sickness and/or disability?

It is therefore not surprising that priests are called upon from time to time to celebrate a funeral Mass for the dead, if the deceased was a baptised Catholic or sometimes to offer a Mass for the dead whether or not the deceased was a Catholic. This has been a known practice from time immemorial.

As no one can claim that he or she has control over the natural death of a human being, what Catholics see thereof as most crucial to do when a family member, a friend or even an enemy has died and is to be prepared for burial, or has already been buried, is to organise prayer sessions for the deceased. The highest form of all prayers, as earlier indicated, is the celebration of the Holy Eucharist. In addition to this, ample opportunities are also created by the bereaved family members for other fervent prayers to be said for God's forgiveness of the sins committed by the deceased.

This is the centre point that drives all arrangements for Christian funeral ceremonies, Thanksgiving Masses and the Reception programmes that follow thereafter. It is good for Catholics themselves to know this and reflect in a Will, as to how one's funeral should be organised, including the way in which continuous prayers should be said for one after the good Lord has called one to his or her final place of rest.

The reflection here undoubtedly reveals some issues that agitate some people's minds during bereavement. It further amplifies the need for elders in the family to periodically discuss with their loved ones, especially with their spouses and children, what to do for them in case of death. For priests and the religious who are not married, they could also leave their last wishes with their superiors and/or local ordinary. This would settle a number of issues that often arise after people have been buried.

It is also important that those among us who have good experience in matters to do with the arrangement of good Christian burials and other prayerful activities that would necessarily follow, should feel free to share this for the benefit of others. It is needless to emphasise that it would also be beneficial if people were to freely present accounts from their own experience in settling the issues that sometimes arise after burial ceremonies of the deceased. It is important to settle any issues between the spouse of the dead and his/her children, between the children and close or distant relations of the dead, or between the children of the dead themselves, as such issues have, in the past, torn many families apart. This will certainly help coming generations to benefit from their wisdom and have guidance on what to do when such situations arise unexpectedly.

It should also be noted here that the sharing of such experience also helps one to fulfil what the scriptures advise us to do as part of our responsibilities, when they state: 'Show yourself in all respects a model of good deeds and in your teaching show integrity, gravity and sound speech that cannot be censured so that an opponent may be put to shame, having nothing evil to say of us' (Ti 2:7–8).

If the messages above from the scriptures are clear enough for us all to take to heart in order to know how to navigate our way through this world to prevent ourselves and our loved ones from going into hellfire as we exit the same world, then one can conclude this chapter here with Psalm 130 and the prayer composed by St Gertrude. Most Catholics hold these prayers so dearly, and many, especially Catholic priests, recite them during the Office of the Dead. The prayers are as follows:

WATING FOR DIVINE REDEMPTION
PSALM 130
Out of the depths I cry to you, O Lord!
Lord, hear my voice!
Let your ears be attentive
to the voice of my supplication!

If you O Lord, should mark iniquities,
Lord, who could stand?

But there is forgiveness with you,
that you may be feared.

I wait for the Lord, my soul waits,
and in his word I hope;
my soul waits for the Lord
more than watchmen for the morning,

O Israel, hope in the Lord!
For with the Lord, there is mercy,
and with him is plenteous redemption.
And he will redeem Israel from all his iniquity.

Glory be to the Father
and to the Son
and to the Holy Spirit,
As it was in the beginning,
is now and ever shall be,
world without end. Amen.

PRAYER OF ST GERTRUDE
Eternal Father,
I offer Thee the Most Precious Blood
of thy Divine Son, Jesus,
in union with the Masses said
throughout the world today,

for all Holy Souls in Purgatory,
for sinners everywhere,
for sinners in the universal Church,
for those in my own home and in my family.
Amen.

10

Friends Who Come to Our Aid in Life and Death

The importance of having good friends cannot be ruled out in this world. They are needed in the home, even among one's children, in the community, in the Church, in the office, in the marketplace, in school, in foreign lands, etc. Good friends may even be very useful to arrange one's funeral after death. Good friends can come from among lay persons, bishops, priests, religious, etc., without tribe, race, colour, or nationality blurring their vision. They can be very handy in joining one who desires to work for God. What one needs is to avoid having ill-feelings towards anyone. And once you make your actions transparent, many good friends will be there to defend you if others try to stab you in the back.

One can come across some of these good friends in school and/or later as old school mates or some could come from among those who have crossed our path in the Church, in the office, at different local ceremonies or at international conferences. My own experience is that anywhere one goes, one can make good friends, provided one has a good heart towards others. This is why I have never been afraid to hire people who are of a different faith, tribe, social status, political leaning, colour and/or nationality to work for me in the workshop, in the office, or at home as domestic staff.

As I writes this, I can look back at my cook who has served for over seventeen years, my driver of over fifteen years, and my accountant who has worked with me for over twelve years. These three key staff mentioned above are all Muslims. They have all worked conscientiously towards the success of every Christian programme undertaken by myself and my wife under the auspices of the Holy Family Society and the Sir David Osunde Foundation for Persons with Disabilities.

Friends That Are at One's Beck and Call

Another circle of friends that my wife and I have are persons with disabilities. They stand by our family twenty-four hours of the day. There is nothing one calls them for in terms of urgent assignments that they cannot do creditably for one. If nothing else, one can testify that their prayers for one are sharper than a blade, because theirs cut through all the barriers in the way to get straight to the living God who hears the cries of the poor. The Psalmist says: 'This poor man cried, and the Lord heard him' (Ps 34:6). Is there any wonder that their prayers are powerful?

The third category of friends that myself and my family have cultivated over the years and which we have held so dear to our hearts, comes from the priesthood and the religious. There are regular interactions between members of our family and this category of friends either at daily morning Mass, before the lockdown occasioned by the coronavirus pandemic, at different Church activities, on the phone or through WhatsApp messages and emails, and during personal visits. The reader may want to know that my wife and I have a few rooms reserved in our house to accommodate any of these categories of friends who knock at the door from time to time. All the visitors know that they are always welcome at any time throughout the year, whether or not we are present in the house, and provided there are vacant rooms.

These visitors do not only contribute immensely to the development and sustenance of our domestic church, but have also, over the years, become formidable spiritual pillars being used by God in different ways to keep our marriage in good standing, fresh, heathy and prosperous.

Faithful Testimony of Having Bishops, Priests and Religious as Special Friends

We can testify faithfully here that we have had the good fortune of having a number of bishops and priests celebrate private Masses for members of our household in our private chapel. And if a priest is, for instance, spending part of his holidays with my family, we sometimes have the benefit of having the exposition of the Blessed Sacrament for one hour or more during the family devotion. In addition to having visiting priests, we have in the past had a Jesuit priest assigned by his Regional Superior to work with us for both the spiritual and physical development of the structures of the Holy Family Society at its permanent site in Abuja. To enable him to carry out his assignments, he had to stay in our residence for several months. So too we have played host in our home to other reverend fathers and sisters of several congregations that have been assigned to work at different times with the Holy Family Society and the Sir David Osunde Foundation for Persons with Disabilities.

The congregations whose reverend sisters have stayed for three years or more at a time in our residence in Abuja include the Pauline Sisters and the Sisters of the Home Visitors of Mary. In the case of the Pauline Sisters, they needed a soft landing in Abuja when they first arrived in the Federal Capital city. They accepted the humble accommodation our family provided them before they moved into a more spacious accommodation in preparation to build their own magnificent residence in Abuja. Three reverend sisters from the Congregation of the Holy Family Sisters of the Needy who were assigned to work for our foundation stayed for three years in our second home in Benin City. This is being mentioned here because of the spiritual benefits that accrued to all members of our family during their stay in our residences. The more important reason for mentioning this is to encourage other families to be ready to play host to reverend fathers and sisters in urban and rural communities whenever the need arises. They can be very helpful in the development of one's family spirituality.

The reader may want to know that our grandchildren learnt how to serve Mass and sing the Latin verses at Vesper in our private chapel as we occasionally had Mass, Family Holy Hour devotion and Benediction in our private chapel. It is needless to re-emphasise here that the priests and reverend sisters who have made our house their home contribute immensely to our own spiritual development and how we see the world through the eyes of persons with disabilities.

Apart from the three categories of friends mentioned above, which we have in and outside Nigeria, we also have another category of friends we sometimes meet once in three years. This is when we attend the triennial World Meeting of Families, held in a large city with sufficient conference and catering facilities. The Vatican, which sponsors and reconvenes the international event, approves the city hosting it on a shifting basis, from one continent to the other. Our interactions both in and outside the conferences give us hope that a lot can still be done by people of the same faith working in collaboration with others from different continents, to make the world a better place to live in. The commitments of individuals to go back to our various countries to become agents of change are always overwhelming.

It may be necessary to point out here that from the reports in Chapters Five, Six and Seven in Volume Two of this book, regarding the participation of our family members in the World Meeting of Families, the reader will discover that being present in such a gathering provides ample opportunities for the participants to make international friends from different parts of the world. It is in such a gathering that one can really appreciate the marvellous work of God in creating human beings and distributing us to different parts of the continents, making everyone in their different areas so unique.

To crown it all, he ensured that we all have our special gifts from him as he made us in his own image and likeness. God did not mince words when he said: 'Let us make man in our image, after our likeness, and let them have dominion over the fish of the sea, and over the birds of the air, and over the cattle, and over all the earth, and over every creeping thing that creeps on the earth' (Gn 1:26). The human being is superb. God made us so. We therefore have no reason to believe that one human being is superior to the other. And there should be no discrimination among us if we really mean to serve and worship God in spirit and in truth. This is the beginning point for any true Christian.

The Undeserved Authority Given to Human Beings
One can see the undeserved authority God gave to us as human beings, and the numerous gifts that he also wholeheartedly embedded in us, given on a platter of gold from birth, by being made in his image and likeness. In addition to these, he gives everyone the freedom to search within our own being for other special gifts, unique to each individual; he gives us the freedom to know them, appreciate them, and make good and profitable use of them all. God has assured us that whatever special gifts in us that we discover by ourselves and thereafter use appropriately, we have his promise that we will receive more gifts from him. This is why Christ said: 'For to everyone who has will more be given, and he will have abundance, but from him who has not, even what he has will be taken away' (Mt 25:29). To drum this message into our ears, St Luke also confirmed this in Luke 19:26.

This should really make us appreciate what we have as special gifts from God and also find time always to thank him for the parts with which he made us individually. The Psalmist recognised this when in his thanksgiving to God he acclaimed: 'For you formed my inward parts; you knitted me together in my mother's womb. I praise you for I am wonderfully made. Wonderful are your works' (Ps 139:13–14). The words of the Psalmist should make us understand and appreciate what God has done in our individual lives. We should also see this as a great encouragement that should propel us to always make the best use of the special gifts imbedded in us by God as we were being formed in the wombs of our mothers.

The most important of all these gifts is the gift of life. There is no doubting the fact that we hear reports of those who went to bed but did not wake up. There are also daily reports of those who die in hospitals. The coronavirus pandemic has even worsened the situation as thousands die every day in the world. And there are everyday reports of those who have died as a result of accidents on the roads or in plane crashes. Do we therefore not consider it that it is by God's amazing grace and his loving kindness that, in spite of our unworthiness, we are still alive?

The Unique Gifts From Our Loving God

Our loving God, having given every human being he created very unique gifts that are different from those given to others, it behoves each person in the world to discern how best his or her gifts could be used profitably to make this world a better place for others and for the coming generations. This is when we can secure even more unique gifts from God. Our ability to deal with fellow human beings whether in our local community or on an international level, with a view to bringing us all nearer to our God, becomes our own individual credit.

This is why it is important for us to know that if we have the unique opportunity to attend any conference where God is placed at the centre of activities, we should use it profitably to make good friends, especially those who can help us to develop our relationship with our God.

Two Lessons to Teach Our Children

One must therefore emphasise here that there are two lessons that we should teach our children and grandchildren. They need to learn how to discern God's gifts imbedded in them and how to make good friends and stick to them always, with a view to using their positive interactions with them to develop and sustain their domestic church. Be quite sure that if our children and grandchildren learn these lessons at home, they will then understand the need to carefully choose their friends even in schools or in their places of work.

And if they act accordingly to what they learn from the domestic church, they will certainly ride high spiritually, become good citizens, and make their parents and grandparents very proud of them. This will show everyone that they are from a well-ordered home and have made effective use of their domestic church. It will also show that the sacrifices that the children and grandchildren themselves have made from day to day to learn new things about how to do ordinary things in an extraordinary manner for the purpose of bringing joy and succour to the lives of others, have been abundantly blessed by God as they yield abundant fruits.

Learning Christian Principles to Help Develop the Domestic Church

As indicated earlier, it is important that everyone in the household has a good grasp of certain Christian principles, some of which could be learnt from our friends. Such knowledge can help us to develop our domestic church. So, exchanging ideas with friends one meets at conferences, either in local or international settings, can help a great deal in advancing our family spirituality. It is for us not to forget our chance meetings with new Christian and non-Christian friends that it becomes very important for us to document these in photographs, and then exchange addresses and phone numbers to enable us to continue building on the new friendship that God has placed on our way.

In international events, such as the World Meeting of Families, one is always amazed to see how people from other continents rush to take photographs with one, either because of one's national dress, the Christian love of sharing good things with one another, or the need to cultivate new Christian friendships, with a view to making the world a better place for all of us to live in.

Historic Pictures of Great Local and International Events

Having now understood the need to build good relationships with others as we strive towards holiness and have a more peaceful environment in our community and in our world at large, it will also be good to share from time to time what binds us together. This can be in the form of music, religious articles, project initiatives, books, historic pictures, etc. If small gifts of this nature are not shared from time to time, we may completely forget our chance meetings with each other. It is for us not to forget our historic meetings at local events and the World Meeting of Families that I have decided to publish in Appendix C a number of the historic pictures taken in Nigeria, Cameroon, Dublin in Ireland in 2018 and Philadelphia in the USA in 2015.

While urging the reader to spend some time praying for the people you see in these pictures, please note that we need to maintain genuine friendships with people, no matter their colour, race, language, status in life, form of disabilities, etc, to make our own lives easygoing, fruitful and focused on winning eternal life together with our loved ones. This should be our goal.

It is hoped that, after seeing the pictures, the reader would be motivated to plan with his or her family members to be participants at the next event or any future international events organised by the Vatican to bring world families together as one unique family of God. This is the main purpose of placing these pictures in Appendix C of this Volume Three. Happy viewing.

NOTE: For the benefit of those who want to participate in the future activities of the Holy Family Society which greatly help people to prepare for the World Meeting of Families as well as bring about the development of their domestic church, it is advisable that you contact the National Secretarial through her email: hfsnationalsecretariat@yahoo.com.

11

Revisiting the Topics in Volumes One, Two and Three and Standing Up for Family Evangelisation

This is to quickly call to mind the main topics that I have reflected on in the three volumes of this book. This is being done in the hope that those who read the contents of the three volumes of this work on the domestic church will have the urge to revive and promote the domestic church, as well as do what is humanly possible to sustain their own, and at the same time, get themselves ready for the new evangelisation mission. By highlighting in this book the spiritual benefits that one can secure in having a functioning domestic church, what becomes obvious to the Christian is that he or she needs to, first and foremost, attribute the correct meaning to the purpose of his or her creation by God.

As I have observed, many do have the unique opportunity of having grandparents or parents to prepare themselves spiritually from the comfort of their homes, coupled with the assistance of the Church, to receive the sacraments of baptism, penance and confirmation. There are others also, like this author, who had to struggle on their own to learn the rudiments of the faith without the assistance of grandparents or parents. This many of them had to do in order to understand the purpose for which God created them.

Let it therefore be clear that in whatever way the opportunity to become a Christian presents itself, one still needs to take the plunge, preferably in one's growing years, to cling on to Christ in order to attain the spiritual strength, wisdom, courage and the love of God that is required to carry out faithfully whatever assignments he has in stock for one in this world.

It should be understood from the beginning that when one decides early to take the bull by the horn to carry out God's assignments, one must at the same time be preparing for a holy death since no one knows when death will knock at the door. Every faithful servant of the Lord must therefore do what is humanly possible to be in the right relationship with the Lord as he or she aspires to return to the warm embrace of the Lord in heaven at his or her demise. This is the faith-building, life-saving message that the reader will discover by spending quality time reading the contents of the three volumes of this book.

To get this message to the hearts of everyone I had to reflect on various topics in the three volumes of this work. My beginning point in Volume One was to bring to the foreknowledge of the reader the reasons why the Holy Family Society, which I founded in the Great Jubilee Year 2000, has taken the challenge to be in the forefront of the new evangelisation mission to re-emphasise the importance of promoting and sustaining the domestic church for the spiritual benefit of every member of one's household. I thereafter brought out certain Christian principles that we need to learn, imbibe and put into practice as we evangelise our families, before going out to evangelise other families.

To recall the points made in my reflections, we are now going to look back at the topics covered in the three volumes of this work. This is being done to refresh the reader's memory, assuming that he or she has already spent quality time going through and digesting the contents of the three volumes. But in case the reader has only read this volume, it is still not too late to secure the first two volumes and read them, as well as pass them over to some other members of your family, as they will greatly help to develop your family spirituality and make your domestic church more functional.

So, the review of Volumes One and Two here will go a long way to give a bird's eye view of the books' contents to the reader, believing that this will encourage him or her to read them in detail. The reader should be happy, for instance, to read and understand why thousands of families spend huge amounts of money every three years to attend the World Meetings of Families sponsored by the Vatican for families to learn something new on how to care for their domestic churches. The reader will also get to understand why people participate effectively in the mission of the Church as well as in world affairs, as they engage themselves in doing ordinary things in extraordinary manners for the purpose of winning eternal life.

Taking this as one of the reasons to read the earlier two volumes, it will not be out of place to state here that whatever the reader finds interesting, insightful and instructive in the three volumes of these works on the domestic church needs to be shared with others, particularly with members of his or her household. Such sharing goes a long way in making people understand the scriptures more and put into action what is learnt daily. This, understandably, prompts more people to strive towards holiness, makes the world a better place and by the grace of God, helps many people to secure eternal life at the time of their exit from this world.

If the purpose of publishing the three volumes of this book on the same subject, and having them come out at the same time is already understood, it will also be interesting to know that their availability will allow them to be used as resource materials in homes, schools, seminaries, workshops, retreats, conferences, etc. It is needless therefore to state that they could be used by parents, grandparents, catechists, teachers, seminarians, elders, etc., to teach different categories of people in the homes, in the Church, in the seminaries or as reference materials during conferences, workshops and seminars.

While Volume One lays bare the preparatory ground for the development of faith in the domestic church, Volumes Two and Three have been written to help the reader to reflect deeply on issues on a higher ground, of our mission on earth and what is to be done by us individually and collectively in order to be where our Lord Jesus Christ wants us to be when our stay in this world has ended.

It is to bring this message to every doorstep that I set my gaze on the subject of the Domestic Church and the New Evangelisation mission, which is the title of Volume One. This subject has been the preoccupation of the Holy Family Society, which I co-founded with my wife twenty years ago. As both of us were appointed by Pope Benedict XVI (now Emeritus) to be members of the Pontifical Council For the Family, we have been actively involved in the new evangelisation mission of the Church.

So, taking a look back to all the important spiritual activities we have been fully engaged in, both locally and internationally, I, in agreement with my wife, felt that the lockdown on the whole world following the coronavirus pandemic providentially created the appropriate time for us to reflect on the domestic church, and encourage families to have functioning domestic churches. It is the result of these joint reflections that I came up with the following topics for Volume One:

(a) how the Holy Family Society, which is currently engaged in the new evangelisation came into existence and its faith-building projects

(b) why the Holy Family Society's mission is to return families to God

(c) why the family as a domestic church requires daily spiritual development

(d) the need to prepare family members for the journey of faith

(e) the need to sustain the domestic church and the roles of family members

(f) the need to teach Christian values and promote them in the domestic church

(g) what to learn in the domestic church for family evangelisation

(h) making good friends to help develop one's domestic church

(i) review of Volume One and preview of Volumes Two and Three, promotion of family holy hour and Holy Family Society songs

Contents of Volumes Two and Three

The reader will notice that Volume Two essentially deals with the need to have a functioning domestic church. It also highlights the importance of attending the World Meeting of Families, with a view to developing our domestic church.

On the other hand, this Volume Three, as the reader must have noticed, places great emphasis on the promotion of holiness in the family. All the topics dealt with in this volume are meant to help grandparents and parents take on the responsibility of encouraging the people in their household to pray more, study the bible more, share more of their experiences together, and act more in positive directions that will result in family members doing ordinary things in extraordinary manners, just as many of those who have been canonised as saints did in their own time.

The reflection on sainthood in Chapter Five of this volume is to encourage the reader to learn more about the lives of the saints, with a view to discovering how the lives of certain married men and women who lived in this world in the past attracted the attention of the Church, to be chosen for canonisation as saints.

It is hoped therefore that when married couples get to know more about sainthood, they will take their marital vocation more seriously by making effective use of their domestic church, since it has been shown that when grandparents, children, grandchildren and other members of the extended family come together to pray frequently, it helps greatly in the development of their family spirituality. In such a home where God is always present in the midst of the praying family, .

many good stories begin to emerge, about favours received from God, or God's call on people to make amends in their own lives and embrace new vocations such as the priesthood or religious life.

Fear of the unknown is banished from such family members because God is always in control of their individual lives. Therefore, they need not be afraid to prepare for a holy death at any time God calls on any one of them. This is what is to be deduced from this my reflection in this particular volume.

So, my reflections on the various topics are meant to prompt the reader to look at the higher gains that come from the individual response to the universal call to holiness and the steadfast struggle that should be in place to bring those who do God's will here on earth to the narrow gate from which they can joyfully gain entrance into heaven. Families are also expected to deduce from the reflections that it is undoubtedly a higher spiritual gain, and a thing of great joy to have a priest and/or reverend sister coming out of a well-ordered Christian home where the domestic church has been very functional in the transmission of faith to its members.

To amplify this message and encourage people to endeavour to have well-ordered Christian homes, the reader has been further introduced to certain fundamentals that can help families make their domestic church not only functional but also successful in preparing members of their own families for effective Christian mission in God's vineyard.

I do not find it out of place to make the audience know that as we struggle every day to attend to our family issues, as well as participate in Church activities and societal duties, we must at the same time take valuable steps to prepare ourselves for a holy death. I would indicate that it is only when we effectively prepare for this that we will find ourselves ready to be welcomed by the Holy Family in heaven when our own time is up here on earth. To justify the position of the scriptures and the Church in these matters, as well as the reason for the Holy Family Society to adopt the same stance, I found it necessary to make references to relevant passages in the bible to drive this message home.

In summary, the topics dwelt on in Volumes Two and Three, which the reader may have read already, include the following:

Volume Two:
The Family as a Domestic Church: Experiences From the World Meeting of Families

Taking Up Your Cross and Following Jesus

Having taken the reader's mind back to the topics that my wife and I had quality time to reflect on in the three volumes of this book, it is worthwhile to state here that anyone who really wants to join the new evangelisation mission of bringing members of his or her family and others back to God must be ready to take up his or her cross every day to follow our Lord, Jesus Christ. He himself told us in a very plain language that, 'he who does not take his cross and follow me is not worthy of me' (Mt 10:38). Having known this, the evangeliser must be ready to join the sufferings and/or disappointments he or she will encounter from time to time in the field with the sufferings of Christ. This is where the evangeliser can lighten their load of sufferings and have a wellspring of happiness, even when he or she is derided or ridiculed.

He or she should also know from the beginning that the disappointments and shocks they will receive in the field will come most likely from family members, close friends, people from his or her community, or people in authority. Christ himself faced such disappointments and the resultant sufferings during his three-year mission on earth. He was not afraid of death. He bowed to his Father's will.

The Sufferings in Stock for the Evangeliser

So, it should not surprise the committed evangeliser that certain sufferings are in stock for him or her. It is because of this that St Paul, in his letter to the Corinthians, said in 1 Corinthians 4:9–13:

> For it seems to me that God has exhibited us apostles, as last of all, like men sentenced to death, because we have become a spectacle to the world, to angels and to men. We are fools for

Christ but you are wise in Christ. We are weak, you are strong. You are held in honour but we in disrepute. To the present hour, we hunger and taste, we are poorly clothed and buffeted and homeless, and we labour, working with our own hands. When reviled, we bless; when persecuted, we endure; when slandered, we try to conciliate; we have become, and are now as the refuse of the world, the dregs of all things.

It is because our forefathers in faith, including Pope St John Paul II, knew that the committed evangelisers would face all these that they warned in advance that in spite of the challenges, sufferings and disappointments lined up along the way, one should never be afraid in carrying out God's assignments. This explains why St Paul in his Letter to the Ephesians, and by extension, to all evangelisers, instructed that everyone must 'be strong in the Lord and in the strength of his might'. He also advised the evangelisers to 'Put on the whole armour of God that you may be able to stand against the wiles of the devil' (Eph 6:10–11). Even when the devil rears his ugly head, Christ admonished us: 'Do not fear those who kill the body but cannot kill the soul; rather fear him who can destroy both soul and body in hell' (Mt 10:28).

Entertain No Fear for God's Work
Therefore, for one to be effective in doing God's work, one is advised not to entertain any fear, instead, one should always strive to gain spiritual strength by listening frequently to the Word of God. This is to be followed up by taking positive action on issues that will help the evangeliser to bring people nearer to God.

As people do testify from time to time, the devoted evangeliser understandably needs to re-energise themselves frequently by receiving the body and blood of Jesus Christ in Holy Communion. He or she must also be ready to share with others the gifts of God that will come their way as they continue with this work. Anyone who is consistent in being an active participant in this evangelical work finds themself also working happily in advance for a holy death, which could come at any time as indicated in Chapters Seven and Eight of this particular volume.

One crucial point that needs to be emphasised here is that whatever sufferings, disappointments and/or shocks one experiences for being an active labourer in God's vineyard 'are not worth comparing with the glory that is to be revealed to us' (Rm 8:18). This should encourage us all to be ready to serve and worship God in spirit and in truth by being ready to face the vicissitudes of life. When we listen to the inner voice through which the Holy Spirit speaks to us, virtually on a daily basis, our holy desire should be to respond positively and correctly to the messages received.

Listening to the Inner Voice of God

All that one is required to do here is to bend low to hearken to the advice of the Psalmist who says: 'O that today you would listen to his voice! Harden not your hearts' (Ps 95:7–8). It is quite possible to be in a position to always listen to the inner voice if we let God dwell perpetually in our hearts. And the surest way of achieving this is when we make great efforts to always be in a state of grace as we make ourselves available for the frequent reception of the Holy Eucharist at Mass.

Being a regular, active participant at Mass is also an essential ingredient for the strengthening of our faith in preparation for one's evangelical work. It is important therefore that those who have accepted the call to join the bandwagon of evangelisers participate actively at Mass, virtually on a daily basis.

The Beauty of the Catholic Church

For those among them who would like to use this book to evangelise effectively, I have decided to reproduce the Order of Mass in Appendix A below. It is hoped that such evangelisers will faithfully utilise the opportunity of being in the presence of the Lord to gain some spiritual benefits, as the Order of Mass makes it possible for active participation, even if the language being used is different from the ones used here. This is the beauty of the Catholic Church, because the Order of Mass is the same everywhere in the world, making it quite easy for everyone to follow from beginning to end.

Meanwhile, I would like to invite the reader, whether or not you are a Catholic, to go to a quiet corner and reflect on what has been genuinely discussed in the ten chapters of this volume to enable you decide what you really want to do with your life. If your decision is to follow Christ, I recommend that your beginning point is to be an active participant at Mass in whatever city or community you live in at this point in time. You could make your individual resolution today that at your earliest opportunity, you will attend Mass at the nearest Catholic Church to your present residence or workplace. To ensure that the reader is not lacking in the knowledge of what makes the Catholic Church unique in her celebration of the Holy Eucharist, the Order of Mass reproduced below will be of great advantage.

Spiritual Benefits of Being a Regular Mass Goer

Let it be clear here that as the reader or the evangelist continues to make the sacrifice to go to Mass every day, they will be surprised to observe the growth in their spiritual development, especially when their interest disengages from the frivolous things in life. It will also be an added advantage in their spiritual growth if they make themselves available to pay frequent visits to the Blessed Sacrament where all worries, anxieties, successes and progress in life can be left at the feet of Jesus who is really present in the consecrated host. It is to be noted here that our Lord Jesus Christ draws regular visitors to the Blessed Sacrament closer to himself.

How can this happen, the inquisitive Christian and non-Christian alike may want to ask here? This can be briefly explained by letting the reader know that Jesus' love for humanity is overwhelming. He wants us to live perpetually in peace, hence the first few words he uttered and shared with the Apostles, and by extension, with all of us, after his resurrection were: 'Peace be with you' (Jn 20:19).

It is this same peace that he extends to us every day as we visit him in the Blessed Sacrament. And his manifest presence there is not in doubt since it is the consecrated host that Christ describes as his own body that is placed there in the tabernacle.

Before the priest places the consecrated host in the tabernacle, he goes through the spiritual ceremony that Christ instituted at the Last Supper. To assure his Apostles and indeed all of us that he was not going to leave us as orphans, Christ instituted the Holy Eucharist in the presence of his Apostles as 'he took bread, and when he had given thanks, broke it and gave it to them, saying, "This is my body which is given for you. Do this in remembrance of me." And likewise the chalice after supper, saying, "This chalice which is poured out for you is the new covenant in my blood"' (Lk 22:19–20).

The Steward of the Mystery of God

The anointed priest of God who is also regarded 'as servant of Christ and steward of the mystery of God' (1 Cor 4:1), has the power flowing from Christ himself to perform this ceremony to make Christ truly present in the consecrated host placed in the tabernacle. This is why Christ is there waiting for us to visit him every day to leave our worries and anxieties at his feet. He invites us to come to him when he says, 'Come to me, all who labour and are heavy laden, and I will give you rest. Take my yoke upon you and learn from me; for I am gentle and lowly in heart, and you will find rest for your souls. For my yoke is easy and my burden light' (Mt 11:28–30).

To further assure us that he is there to attend to our needs, he says, 'Ask it will be given to you; seek and you will find; knock, it will be opened to you. For everyone who asks receives, and he who seeks, finds, and for him who knocks, it will be opened' (Mt 7:7–8).

God Fills the Desire of Those Who Fear Him

If we believe this and take our problems to our Lord Jesus Christ, the scriptures also assure us that: 'No one who believes in him will be put to shame' (Rm 10:11). In the same scriptures, we learn that 'the Lord is near to all who call upon him, to all who call upon him in truth. He fills the desire of all who fear him, he also hears their cry and saves them' (Ps 145:18–19). It is therefore my recommendation that those who believe in Jesus Christ should make it a habit to always find time to visit him in the Blessed Sacrament, more so as Christ further reveals himself to us, when he says, 'I am the light of the world; he who follows me will not walk in darkness, but will have the light of life' (Jn 8:12). So, if we allow Jesus to take complete control of our lives and follow his footsteps as we walk along with him, we will be in perpetual light and therefore, we will not experience darkness in our lives.

And if God's light guides our way every day, we can conveniently repel, or unknowingly reduce any form of unsolicited discomfort that may come our way, by making it a habit to always say while visiting the Blessed Sacrament, walking along the road, attending to customers, or relaxing in the comfort of our own homes, that: 'In the Lord I take refuge' (Ps 11:1). This is a very important habit to cultivate because the life of a good Christian is usually marked by the pains and sufferings some aggrieved people, including some trusted friends, may wish to inflict upon him or her.

Leaning Comfortably on Jesus Christ

The other reason we need to follow Jesus, walk along with him and be in his presence all the time, whether we are at home, in the Church, in the school, in the marketplace or on the road is that he says to us at every point in time: 'I am the Way and the Truth and the Life; no one comes to the father, but by me' (Jn 14:6). If we know this, it becomes very instructive that we should lean on him who will eventually take us to his Father in heaven.

So, for us to contemplate Jesus all the time and be in his presence, we need to help ourselves by having certain spiritual tools that can help us to contemplate him individually and collectively, and also feel his presence. It is to enable us to do this from time to time, especially when we are in the presence of the Blessed Sacrament, that I am also reproducing the prayers that family members can use when they are before the Blessed Sacrament. These same prayers can be used in the domestic church where there is no opportunity to have exposition of the Blessed Sacrament.

Family Holy Hour

What we need to realise is that Christ himself has assured us that 'where two or three are gathered in my name, there am I in their midst' (Mt 18:20). This makes it important for family members to always come together to pray in their private chapel or in a place designated for prayers in their homes. Apart from the usual family prayers that family members say at home, they could also have some days set apart for everyone to have Family Holy Hour Devotion. It is to help promote this devotion that we have included the prayers specially compiled by Rev. Fr Ed Debany, SJ, for family use. This is also reproduced in Appendix A of this volume. Immediately following this is Appendix B, which features some selected Holy Family Society songs dedicated to the Holy Family of Nazareth that I have composed. They are taken from the Song Book I have previously published.

Feast of the Holy Family,
27 December 2020, Miami, Florida
Sir David E. Osunde
Founder/National Coordinator, Holy Family Society

Appendices

Appendix A
ORDER OF MASS

INTRODUCTORY RITES

ENTRANCE PROCESSION

As the celebrant enters, the entrance hymn is sung by the people or choir, then the priest goes to the Altar and makes the customary reverence with the ministers, kisses the Altar and (if incense is used) incenses the Altar.

ENGLISH
C. In the name of the Father and of the Son and of the Holy Spirit.
P. Amen.

LATIN
C. In nomine Patris et Filii, et Spiritus Sancti.
P. Amen.

GREETING

ENGLISH
C. The grace of our Lord Jesus Christ, and the love of God, and the Communion of the Holy Spirit be with you all.
P. And with your spirit.

LATIN
C. Gratia Domini nostri Iesu Christi, et Caritas Dei, et Communicatio Sancti Spiritus Sit cum omnibus vobis.
P. Et cum spiritu tuo.

PENITENTIAL RITE

(1) ENGLISH
C. Brethren (brothers and sisters), let us acknowledge our sins, and so prepare ourselves to celebrate the sacred mysteries.

LATIN
C. Fratres, agnoscamus peccata nostra, ut apti simus ad sacra mysteria celebranda.

After a brief silence all say: (confiteor)

ENGLISH
P. I confess to Almighty God and to you, my brothers and sisters, that I have greatly sinned in my thoughts and in my words, in what I have done and in what I have failed to do, through my fault, through my fault, through my most grievous fault; therefore I ask Blessed Mary ever-Virgin, all the angels and saints, and you, my brothers and sisters, to pray for me to the Lord our God. Amen.

LATIN

C. Confiteor Deo Ominipotenti et vobis, fratres, quia peccavi nimis cogitatione, verbo, opere et omissione: mea culpa, mea culpa, mea maxima culpa. Ideo precor beatam Mariam semper Virginem, omnes Angelos et Sanctos, et vos fratres, orare pro me ad Dominum Deum nostram.

ENGLISH

C. May Almighty God have mercy on us, forgive us our sins, and bring us to everlasting life.

P. Amen.

LATIN

C. Misereatur nostri, omnipotens Deus et, dimissis peccatis nostris, perducat nos ad vitam aeternam.

P. Amen.

(2) ENGLISH

C. You were sent to heal the contrite of heart: Lord, have mercy.

P. Lord, have mercy.

C. You came to call sinners: Christ, have mercy.

P. Christ, have mercy.

C. You are seated at the right hand of the Father to intercede for us: Lord, have mercy.

P. Lord, have mercy.

C. May almighty God have mercy on us, forgive us our sins, and bring us to everlasting life.

P. Amen.

LATIN

C. Qui missus es sanare contritos corde: Kyrie, eleison.

P. Kyrie, eleison.

C. Qui peccatores vocare venisti: Christe, eleison.

P. Christe, eleison.

C. Qui ad dexteram Patris sedes, ad interpellandum pro nobis: Kyrie, eleison

P. Kyrie, eleison.

C. Misereatur nostri omnipotens Deus et, dimissis peccatis nostris, perducat nos ad vitam aeternam.

P. Amen.

The Kyrie Eleison (Lord, have mercy) invocations follow, unless they have just occurred in a formula of the penitential Act.

ENGLISH
C. Lord, have mercy
P. Lord, have mercy

C. Christ, have mercy
P. Christ, have mercy

C. Lord, have mercy
P. Lord, have mercy

LATIN
C. Kyrie, Eleison
P. Kyrie, Eleison

C. Christe, eleison
P. Christe, eleison

C. Kyrie, Eleison
P. Kyrie, Eleison

At the end of the prayer, the people respond:
P. Amen

(The Gloria is sung or said by the celebrant or the choir)

ENGLISH

Glory to God in the highest, and on earth peace to people of goodwill. We praise you, we bless you, we adore you, we glorify you, we give you thanks for your great glory, Lord God, heavenly King, O God, almighty Father. Lord Jesus Christ, Only Begotten Son, Lord God, Lamb of God, Son of the Father, you take away the sins of the world, have mercy on us; you take away the sins of the world, receive our prayer; you are seated at the right hand of the Father, have mercy on us. For you alone are the Holy One, you alone are the Lord, you alone are the Most High, Jesus Christ, with the Holy Spirit, in the glory of God the Father. Amen.

LATIN

Gloria in excelsis Deo et in terra pax hominibus bonae voluntatis. Laudamus te, benedicimus te, adoramus te, glorificamus te, gratias agimus tibi propter magnam gloriam tuam, Domine Deus, Rex caelestis, Deus Pater omnipotens. Domine Fili unigenite, Iesu Christe, Domine Deus, Agnus Dei, Filius Patris, qui tollis peccata mundi, miserere nobis; qui tollis peccata mundi, suscipe deprecationem nostram. Qui sedes ad dexteram Patris, miserere nobis. Quoniam tu solus Sanctus, tu solus Dominus, tu solus Altissimus, Iesu Christe, cum Sancto Spiritu: in gloria Dei Patris. Amen.

COLLECT

ENGLISH
C. Let us pray.

LATIN
C. Oremus.

THE LITURGY OF THE WORD

After the prayer/collect, the lector or reader goes to the lectern for the First and Second Readings. After each reading:

ENGLISH
R. The Word of the Lord.
P. Thanks be to God.

LATIN
R. Verbum Domini.
P. Deo gratias.

Before the Gospel, the Alleluia is intoned by the reader or choir and is joined by all. Then, the celebrant goes to the lectern to proclaim the Gospel while all stand.

ENGLISH
C. The Lord be with you.
P. And with your spirit.
C. A reading from the Holy Gospel According to N.
P. Glory to you, O Lord.

LATIN
C. Dominus vobiscum.
P. Et cum spiritu tuo.
C. Lectio sancti Evangelii secundum N.
P. Gloria tibi, Domine.

(At the end of the Gospel)

ENGLISH
C. The Gospel of the Lord.
P. Praise to you, Lord Jesus Christ.

LATIN

C. Verbum Domini.

P. Laus tibi, Christe.

The homily follows. After the homily, there is a brief silence before the Creed.

THE PROFESSION OF FAITH

ENGLISH

I believe in one God, the Father almighty, maker of heaven and earth, of all things visible and invisible. I believe in one Lord Jesus Christ, the only Begotten Son of God, born of the Father before all ages. God from God, Light from Light, true God from true God, begotten, not made, consubstantial with the Father; through him all things were made. For us men and for our salvation he came down from heaven, (here all bow) and by the Holy Spirit was incarnate of the Virgin Mary, and became man. For our sake he was crucified under Pontius Pilate, he suffered death and was buried, and rose again on the third day in accordance with the Scriptures. He ascended into heaven and is seated at the right hand of the Father. He will come again in glory to judge the living and the dead and his kingdom will have no end. I believe in the Holy Spirit, the Lord, the giver of life, who proceeds from the Father and the Son, who with the Father and the Son is adored and glorified, who has spoken through the prophets. I believe in one, holy, catholic and apostolic Church. I confess one baptism for the forgiveness of sins and I look forward to the resurrection of the dead and the life of the world to come. Amen.

LATIN

Credo in unum Deum, Patrem omnipotentem, factorem caeli et terrae, visibilium omnium et invisibilium. Et in unum Dominum Iesum Christum, Filium Dei Unigenitum, et ex Patre natum ante omnia saecula. Deum de Deo, lumen de lumine, Deum verum de Deo vero, genitum, non factum, consubstantialem Patri: per quem omnia facta sunt. Qui propter nos homines et propter nostram salutem descendit de caelis. (omnes se inclinant) Et incarnatus est de Spiritu Sancto ex Maria Virgine, et homo factus est. Crucifixus etiam pro nobis sub Pontio Pilato; passus et sepultus est. Et resurrexit tertia die, secundum scripturas, et ascendit in caelum, sedet ad dexteram Patris. Et iterum venturus est cum gloria, iudicare vivo et mortuos, cuius regni non erit finis. Et in Spiritum Sanctum, Dominum et vivificantem: qui ex Patre Filioque procedit. Qui cum Patre et Filio simul adoratur et conglorificatur: qui locutus est per prophetas. Et unam, sanctam, catholicam et apostolicam Ecclesiam. Confiteor unum baptisma in remissionem peccatorum. Et exspecto resurrectionem mortuorum, et vitam venturi saeculi. Amen.

PRAYER OF THE FAITHFUL

The celebrant or a deacon introduces and concludes the prayer. The intentions are said by someone else; after each intention, the people make common response.

LITURGY OF THE EUCHARIST
(PREPARATION OF GIFTS)

ENGLISH
C. Blessed are you, Lord God of all creation, for through your goodness we have received the bread we offer you: fruit of the earth and work of human hands, it will become for us the bread of life.
P. Blessed be God for ever.

C. Blessed are you, Lord God of all creation, for through your goodness we have received the wine we offer you: fruit of the vine and work of human hands, it will become our spiritual drink.
P. Blessed be God for ever.

LATIN

C. Benedictus es, Domine, Deus universi, quia de tua largitate accepimus panem, quem tibi offerimus, fructum terrae et operis manuum hominum: ex quo nobis fiet panis vitae.

P. Benedictus Deus in saecula.

C. Benedictus es, Domine, Deus universi, quia de tua largitate accepimus vinum, quod tibi offerimus, fructum vitis et operis manuum hominum: ex quo nobis fiet potus spiritalis.

P. Benedictus Deus in saecula.

After the Celebrant has washed his hands, he says:

ENGLISH

C. Pray, brethren (brothers and sisters), that my sacrifice and yours may be acceptable to God, the almighty Father.

P. May the Lord accept the sacrifice at your hands for the praise and glory of his name, for our good and the good of all his holy Church.

LATIN

C. Orate fratres, ut meum ac vestrum sacrificium acceptabile fiat apud Deum Patrem omnipotentem.

P. Suscipiat Dominus sacrificium de manibus tuis ad laudem et gloriam nominis sui, ad utilitatem quoque nostram totiusque Ecclesiae suae sanctae.

The celebrant then says the prayer over the gifts. At the end, People respond:

Amen.

ENGLISH
THE EUCHARISTIC PRAYER
C. The Lord be with you.
P. And with your spirit.

C. Lift up your hearts.
P. We lift them up to the Lord.

C. Let us give thanks to the Lord our God.
P. It is right and just.

LATIN
PREX EUCHARISTICA
C. Dominus vobiscum.
P. Et cum spiritu tuo.

C. Sursum corda.
P. Habemus ad Dominum.

C. Gratias agamus Domino Deo nostro.
P. Dignum et iustum est.

The Celebrant then says the appropriate preface. At the end, together with the people, he says:

ENGLISH
Holy, Holy, Holy Lord God of hosts.
Heaven and earth are full of your glory.
Hosanna in the highest.
Blessed is he who comes in the name of the Lord.
Hosanna in the highest.

LATIN

Sanctus, Sanctus, Sanctus Dominus Deus Sabaoth.
Pleni sunt caeli et terra gloria tua.
Hosanna in excelsis.
Benedictus qui venit in nomine Domini.
Hosanna in excelsis.

After the Consecration, the Celebrant says:

ENGLISH
THE MYSTERY OF FAITH
P. (a) We proclaim your Death, O Lord,
And profess your Resurrection
until you come again.

(b) When we eat the Bread and drink this Cup,
we proclaim your Death, O Lord,
until you come again.

(c) Save us, Saviour of the world,
for by your Cross and Resurrection
you have set us free.

LATIN
MYSTERIUM FIDEI
P. (a) Mortem tuam annuntiamus Domine,
et tuam resurrectionem confitemur,
donec venias.

(b) Quotiescumque
manducamus panem hunc
et calicem bibimus, Mortem
tuam annuntiamus, Domine,
donec venias.

(c) Salvator mundi, salva nos,
qui per crucem et
resurrectionem tuam
liberasti nos.

The Celebrant then continues the Eucharistic Prayer. At the end,
he takes the chalice and the paten with the Consecrated Host and
lifting them up, he says:

ENGLISH
C. Through Him, and with Him, and in
Him, to you, O God, almighty Father,
in the unity of the Holy Spirit, is all
honour and glory, forever and ever.
P. Amen

LATIN
C. Per Ipsum, et cum Ipso, et in Ipso
est tibi Deo Patri omnipotenti,
in unitate Spiritus Sancti,
omnis honor et gloria,
per omnia saecula saeculorum.
P. Amen.

COMMUNION RITE

THE LORD'S PRAYER

ENGLISH
C. At the Saviour's command and formed by divine teaching, we
dare to say:

Our Father, who art in heaven, hallowed be thy name; thy
kingdom come, thy will be done on earth as it is in heaven. Give

us this day our daily bread, and forgive us our trespasses, as we forgive those who trespass against us; and lead us not into temptation, but deliver us from evil.

LATIN

C. Praeceptis salutaribus moniti, et divina institutione formati, audemus dicere:

Pater noster, qui est in caelis; sanctificetur nomen tuum; adveniat regnum tuum; Fiat voluntas tua, sicut in caelo, et in terra. Panem nostrum quotidianum, da nobis hodie; et dimitte nobis debita nostra, sicut et nos dimittimus debitoribus nostris; et ne nos inducas in tentationem; sed libera nos a malo.

ENGLISH

C. Deliver us, Lord, we pray, from every evil, graciously grant peace in our days, that, by the help of your mercy, we may be always free from sin and safe from all distress, as we await the blessed hope and the coming our Saviour Jesus Christ.

LATIN

C. Libera nos, quaesumus, Domine, ab omnibus malis, da propitius pacem in diebus nostris, ut, ope misericordiae tuae adiuti, et a peccato simus semper liberi et ab omni perturbatione securi: exspectantes beatam spem et adventum Salvatoris nostri Iesu Christi.

ENGLISH

P. For the kingdom, the power and the glory are yours now and for ever.

LATIN

P. Quia tuum est regnum, et potestas, et gloria in saecula.

ENGLISH
C. Lord Jesus Christ, who said to your Apostles, peace I leave you, my peace I give you, look not on our sins, but on the faith of your Church, and graciously grant her peace and unity in accordance with your will. Who live and reign for ever and ever.
P. Amen.

LATIN
C. Domine Iesu Christe, qui dixisti Apostolis tuis: Pacem relinquo vobis, pacem meam do vobis: ne respicias peccata nostra, sed fidem Ecclesiae tuae, eamque secundum voluntatem tuam pacificare et coadunare digneris. Qui vivis et regnas in saecula saeculorum.
P. Amen.

ENGLISH
C. The peace of the Lord be with you always

LATIN
C. Pax Domini sit semper vobiscum.

ENGLISH
P. And with your spirit.

LATIN
P. Et cum spiritu tuo.

ENGLISH
C. Let us offer each other the sign of peace.

LATIN
C. Offerte vobis pacem.

There may follow an exchange of a sign of peace, according to the local Custom.

BREAKING OF BREAD

During the breaking of bread, the Lamb of God is sung or recited.

ENGLISH

Lamb of God, you take away the sins of the world,
have mercy on us.
Lamb of God, you take away the sins of the world,
have mercy on us.
Lamb of God, you take away the sins of the world,
grant us peace.

LATIN

Agnus Dei, qui tollis peccata mundi,
miserere nobis.
Agnus Dei, qui tollis peccata mundi,
miserere nobis.
Agnus Dei, qui tollis peccata mundi,
dona nobis pacem.

*This may be repeated until the breaking of the bread is finished.
The last phrase is always: Grant us peace.*

*The Celebrant then says quietly, a private prayer before
communion. At the end, he genuflects and takes the Consecrated
Host and says:*

ENGLISH

C. Behold the Lamb of God, behold him who takes away the sins
of the world. Blessed are those called to the supper of the Lamb.

LATIN

C. Ecce Agnus Dei, ecce qui tolis peccata mundi. Beati qui ad cenam
Agni vocati sunt.

ENGLISH
P. Lord, I am not worthy that you should enter under my roof, but only say the word and my soul shall be healed.

LATIN
P. Domine, non sum dignus, ut intres sub tectum meum, sed tantum dic verbo et sanabitur anima mea.

ENGLISH
C. May the body and blood of Christ bring us to everlasting life.
P. Amen.

LATIN
C. Corpus et Sanguis Christi custodiat me in vitam aeternam.
P. Amen.

DISTRIBUTION OF COMMUNION

ENGLISH
C. The body of Christ.
P. Amen.

LATIN
C. Corpus Christi.
P. Amen.

POST COMMUNION PRAYER

ENGLISH
C. Let us pray.

LATIN
C. Oremus.

THE CONCLUDING RITES

ENGLISH
C. The Lord be with you.

LATIN
C. Dominus Vobiscum.

ENGLISH
P. And with your spirit.

LATIN
P. Et cum spiritu tuo.

ENGLISH
C. May Almighty God bless you, the Father, and the Son, and the Holy Spirit.
P. Amen.

LATIN
C. Benedicat vos omnipotens Deus, Pater, et Filius, et Spiritus Sanctus.
P. Amen.

DISMISSAL

ENGLISH
C. Go forth, the Mass is ended.

OR

C. Go and announce the Gospel of the Lord.

LATIN
C. Ite, missa est.
(in Easter, Alleluia is added)

ENGLISH
P. Thanks be to God.

LATIN
P. Deo Gratias.

PRIVATE ADORATION
FAMILY HOLY HOUR WITH BENEDICTION OF THE BLESSED SACRAMENT

EXPOSITION *(In the Church or when a priest is present in a family home to do the exposition.*
Please kneel as the priest exposes the Blessed Sacrament)

Opening Hymn: We Adore You ...
Godhead here in hiding, whom we do adore,
masked by these bare shadows, shape and nothing more;
See Lord at Thy service, low lies here a heart,
Lost are we in wonder, at the God Thou art.

Seeing, touching, tasting, are in thee deceived
How says trusty hearing, that shall be believed.
What God's Son has told me, take for truth I do,
Truth Himself speaks truly, or there's nothing true!

Jesus whom I look at, shrouded here below,
I beseech Thee send me what I thirst for so.
Someday to look upon Thee, face to face in light;
And be blest forever, with Thy glory's sight.

Adore Devote – Latin
Adore Devote, lantes Deitas,
Quae sub his figures vere latitas:
Tibi se cor meum totum subjicit
Qui ad te comtemplans, totum deficit.

Visus, tactus, gustus, in te fallitur
Sed auditu solo, tuto creditur.

Credo quidquid dixit Dei filius:
Nil hoc verbo veri-tatis, verius.

Jesus quem velatum, nunc aspicio,
Oro fiat illud, quid tam sitio:
Ut te revelata cernens facie,
Visus sim beatus, tuae gloriae. Amen.

OPENING PRAYER BEFORE THE BLESSED SACRAMENT

(ALL) Oh Lord Jesus Christ, it is your great Love for mankind that keeps you day and night in this Sacrament, full of pity and love, expecting, inviting and welcoming all who visit you. We believe that you are really present in the Sacrament of the altar. We adore you and thank you for the graces you have given to us as members of the Holy Family Society, especially for the gift of yourself in this Sacrament. We intercede with you for our family members here present – both young and old, healthy and sick – as well as those not physically present with us at this time.

May no worries or distractions keep us from looking upon you most Blessed of all Sacraments. Accept our weariness and tiredness. You who promised to refresh and strengthen all who are burdened and wearied by life's challenges and temptations, refresh us and our family members with your Passion. Help us not to be weary nor to fall asleep as did the Apostles, Peter, James and John, in the Garden of Gethsemane. Help us Lord Jesus, to be alert as we pray for the sanctification of our Church, our nation, Nigeria, and other nations of the world, and especially for the unity and sanctification of our families.

Oh Jesus, Bread of Life, food of angels and of men, may our adoration of you make us a better, more generous and kinder people. May it form us and mould us to act as you once behaved with your Mother Mary and St Joseph, in the Holy Family of Nazareth. Amen.

LITANY OF THE HOLY FAMILY

The Leader chants or recites the Litany. The people respond with: **Have mercy on us**

Leader: Lord have mercy **(Repeat)** + Christ have mercy **(Repeat)** + Lord have mercy **(Repeat)**
Leader: Jesus hear us, **People:** Jesus graciously hear us.
God the Father of Heaven,
(All respond: Have mercy on us),

+ God the Son, Redeemer of the World,

+ God the Holy Spirit,

+ Holy Trinity, One God,

+ Holy Family, model of family life, **(All respond: Pray for us)**

+ Holy Family, most meek, humble and devout,

+ Holy Family, most wise, patient and obedient,

+ Holy Family, most pure, chaste and caring,

+ Holy Family, most faithful, courageous and powerful,

+ Holy Family, most prudent, generous and vulnerable,

+ Abyss of peace, love and unity,

+ Possessor and dispenser of all graces,

+ Freedom of captives and comforter of the afflicted,

+ Help of Christians and Health of the sick,

+ Conversion of sinners and Returner of the exiles,

+ Freedom of the Souls in Purgatory,

+ Victor over demons and powers,

+ Protector and provider of the poor,

+ Comfort of widows and orphans,

+ Power of fertility and safe delivery,

+ Protector and good shepherd of families,

+ Chain binding all couples,

+ End of all battles.

Lamb of God, who takes away the sins of the world, **(Spare us O Lord)**

Lamb of God, who takes away the sins of the world, **(Graciously hear us O Lord)**

Lamb of God, who takes away the sins of the world, **(Have mercy on us)**

Leader: Jesus Christ hear us,
People: Jesus Christ graciously hear us.

Leader: Pray for us O Holy Family.
People: That we may be made worthy of the promises of our God.

(ALL) Almighty Father, you have made the Holy Family of Jesus, Mary and Joseph to be the model of all family life, grant all our families the grace to imitate them so as to please, praise and glorify you and at the end be welcomed into your Kingdom where you live and reign with Jesus and the Holy Spirit, one God for ever and ever. Amen.

PRAYER AGAINST EVIL SPIRITS, FORCES AND TEMPTATIONS!

(ALL) O Sacrament Most Holy, O Sacrament Divine, all praise and all thanksgiving, be every moment thine! Amen. (brief pause).

O God – Father, Son and Holy Spirit, Most Holy Trinity, Immaculate Virgin Mary, Angels, Archangels and Saints of Heaven, descend upon us as we kneel before the Blessed Sacrament of love and healing. Please purify us Lord, mould us, fill us with yourself, use us. Banish all the forces of evil from our families, destroy them, vanquish them so that we may be healthy and do the good deeds we want to do while refusing to do the bad deeds we so detest. Banish from our family members both present and absent all spells, witchcraft, evil spirits, demons, diabolic infestations, oppressions and possessions; all that is evil and sinful – lack of trust, selfishness, disobedience, envy, pride, psychological, moral, spiritual and diabolic ailments. Drive all these evils away from us and our household, that they may not disturb us nor our loved ones. Jesus, whom we look at present upon this altar, we ask that you command all the forces that vex us as family, *to leave us* and to be consigned into everlasting hell where they will be bound by Saint Michael, the Archangel, and crushed under the heel of the Immaculate Virgin Mary, Mother of the Holy Family and Queen of Nigeria. **(Here pause for one minute silent adoration).**

INTERCESSORY PRAYER TO MARY, MOTHER OF THE HOLY EUCHARIST

NOTE: *Here follows the slow, meditative recitation of one decade of the Holy Rosary keeping in mind ten different people or situations that we want to bring to Jesus for his attention. Pray especially for family members most in need of our Lady's intercession.*

Pause briefly between each Hail Mary while also thinking of the person or situation to pray for. This may be followed by Morning or Evening Prayer from the Divine Office Book.

BENEDICTION HYMNS

Down in adoration falling
This Great Sacrament we hail.
Over ancient forms of worship,
Newer rites of Grace prevail,
Faith will tell us Christ is present,
When our human senses fail.

To the Everlasting Father
And the Son who made us free,
And the Spirit, God proceeding
From them each eternally.
Be Salvation, Honour, Blessing
Height and endless Majesty.
Amen.

LATIN

Tantum ergo Sacramentum
Veneremur cernui
Et anticum documentum
Novo cedat ritui
Praestet fides supplementum
Sensuum defectui.

Genitori genitoque
Laus et iubilatio
Salus, Honour, Virtus Quoque
Sit et Benedictio
Procedenti ab utroque
Compar sit laudatio.
Amen.

Priest: Panem de caelo praestitisti eis.
(You have given us Bread from Heaven)
People: Omne delectamentum in se habentem.
(Having all sweetness within it)

Priest: Oremus: Deus, qui nobis sub Sacramentum mirabili
Passionis tuae memoriam reliquisti; tribue quaesumus ita nos
Corporis et Sanguinis tui sacra mysteria venerari, ut
redemptionis tuae fructum in nobis iugiter sentiamus. Qui vivis
et regnas in saecula saeculorum. Amen.

(In English) *Let us pray: Oh Lord our God, you have left us in this
wonderful Sacrament, a memorial of your Passion and Resurrection, help
us we beg you, to reverence the Mystery of your Body and Blood, that we
may always experience the fruits of your Salvation. You who live and
reign for ever and ever. Amen.*

THE DIVINE PRAISES
Blessed be God.
Blessed be His Holy Name.
Blessed be Jesus Christ, true God and true Man.
Blessed be the Name of JESUS.
Blessed be His most Sacred Heart.
Blessed be His most Precious Blood.
Blessed be Jesus Christ, in the most Holy Sacrament of the Altar.
Blessed be the Holy Spirit the Paraclete.

Blessed be the Great Mother of God, Mary most Holy.
Blessed be Her holy and Immaculate Conception.
Blessed be Her Glorious Assumption.
Blessed be the Name of Mary, Virgin and Mother.
Blessed be St Joseph, Her most Chaste Spouse.
Blessed be God in His Angels and in His Saints.

ADOREMUS et LAUDATE (We adore and praise You O Blessed Sacrament)
Priest (only): Adoremus in Aeternum, Sanctissimum Sacramentum.
People: Repeat ...
Priest (only): Laudate Dominum omnes gentes Laudate eum omnes populi.
People: Quoniam confirmata est super nos misericordia eius; et veritas Domini manet in aeternum.
Priest: Gloria Patri et Filio, et Spiritui Sancto
+ Sicut erat in principio, et nunc et semper. et in saecula saeculorum. Amen.
People: Adoremus in Aeternum, Sacramentum, Sanctissimum Sacramentum.

SALVE REGINA (Hail Holy Queen)
Salve Regina, Mater misericordia, Vita dulcedo et spes nostra salve. Ad te clamamus, exules Filii Evae ad te suspiramus, gemente et flentes, in hac lacrimarum valle. Eia ergo, advocata nostra Illos tuos misericordes oculos, ad nos converte, Et Iesum, benedicum fructum ventris tui. Nobis, post hoc exilium ostende, O clemens, O pia, O dulcis Virgo Maria.

Priest: Pray for us O Holy Mother of God.
People: That we may be made worthy of the promises of Christ.

Let us pray: O God, Our refuge and our strength, look down with favour upon your people who cry to you; and by the intercession of the Glorious and Immaculate Virgin Mary, Mother of God, of St Joseph her faithful spouse, of your blessed Apostles, Peter and Paul, and of all the Saints, mercifully and graciously hear the prayers which we pour forth for the conversion of sinners, and for the liberty and exultation of our Holy Mother, the Church, through the same Christ our Lord. Amen.

Our Lady Queen of Nigeria – Pray for us!
Holy Family: Make our family like yours!
Jesus, Mary and Joseph: Protect our family and save the souls of all the faithful departed!
Holy Family: Be our model and our inspiration!

Closing Hymn: Holy Queen We Bend Before Thee
Holy Queen we bend before thee
Queen of purity divine
Make us love thee we implore thee
Make us truly to be thine.

R. Teach, oh teach us Holy Mother how to conquer every sin.
How to love and help each other, how the price of life to win.

Thou to whom a child is given
Greater than the sons of men
Coming down from highest heaven
To create the world again. **R**

NOTE 1: *Other songs, such as those reproduced in Appendix B of this book can also be rendered both at the beginning and at the end of the Family Holy Hour.*

NOTE 2: *Fr Ed Debany, SJ who compiled the prayer for the Family Holy Hour above, was assigned by his Regional Superior to work with the Holy Family Society in 2012, during which time he accompanied this author to attend the Seventh World Meeting of Families that took place in Milan, Italy. He took most of the historic pictures the reader will find in Volumes Two and Three of this book.*

Meanwhile, some historic pictures marking the activities of the Holy Family Society, both at the local and national levels where a number of the topics in this volume are discussed are featured in Appendix C to this volume.

Appendix B
SELECTED HOLY FAMILY SONGS/HYMNS

(May be used after each decade of the Holy Rosary and at Mass)

(1) Jesus, Mary and Joseph

CHORUS:
Jesus, Mary and Joseph – the Holy Family
The Model Family of our world
You are the only one that we know
And you are the only love of our hearts

1. Let us build our home in Jesus, Mary and Joseph
   To experience the presence of God;
   As we make our home a 'Domestic Church'
   Where love is the family's watch word

2. Let us build our home in Christian love
   To pray daily in the presence of God
   As we gather around the table of the Lord
   Where the worthy partakes of His meal

3. Let us unite our families in Christian love
   To share the blessings of the Lord
   As we come before His altar of Grace
   Where everyone is invited to share His gift

4. Let us work together as a family of God
   To build God's Church here on earth
   As we gather the strength, the strength of our parish
   Where love flows among our members

(2) Holy Family, The Mirror

CHORUS:
Holy Family, the mirror for the world
You are our gaze and focus every day
For when we see you in the mirror
You remind us of your sterling virtues
We need your help to be like you
In order to win God's favour
And secure a happy, eternal life

1. Jesus, Mary and Joseph
   Your obedience to the Father
   Teaches us a lot every day
   We humbly ask for your help
   To do God's will
   Never let Your children go astray

2. Jesus, Mary and Joseph
   Your love for the Father
   Teaches us a lot every day
   We humbly ask for your help
   To love the Father the more and more
   Never let Your children go astray

3. Jesus, Mary and Joseph
   Your patience with the Father
   Teaches us a lot every day
   We humbly ask for your help
   To be patient in time of need
   Never let Your children go astray

4. Jesus, Mary and Joseph
   Your care for the poor

Teaches us a lot every day
We humbly ask for your help
To care for our neighbour
Never let Your children go astray

(3) Fathers and Mothers

CHORUS:
Fathers and mothers
Get your children together to praise the Lord
To praise the Lord,
To praise the Lord, for his love and mercy
For our own good health
And for our peace at home

1. Let us come together
   As a family of God
   To pray and to dance
   For we, we are one

2. Let us make sign of the cross
   As Catholics
   On our forehead
   To begin our prayer

3. Let us bow our heads
   In humble submission
   And reflect in our hearts
   The holy and noble virtues

4. Let us dance with joy
   In praise to our God
   For sparing our own lives
   For His purpose on earth

5. Praise the Father, the Son and Holy Spirit
   Both now and forever more
   The God who was, who is, and who will be
   For ages unending, Amen.

(4) Knowing Jesus, Mary and Joseph

CHORUS:

Knowing Jesus, Mary and knowing Joseph,
Is my joy every day, every day
Knowing the Holy Family is the joy of my family,
Knowing the Holy Family of Nazareth,
Is what we must do
To have joy in our heart,
And joy in our home.

1. Every day, I take time to read the scripture
   To know more about the Holy Family
   What about you my dear friend?

2. Every day, my family reflects
   On the virtues of Jesus, Mary and Joseph
   What about you my dear friend?

3. Every day, I struggle to practice
   The virtues of the Holy Family
   What about you my dear friend?

4. Every day, I depend on the Holy Family
   To improve my own spirituality
   What about you my dear friend?

5. Every day, I call on the Holy Family
   To show me the way to the Father
   What about you my dear friend?

6. Every day, I kneel down to bless
   The Holy Family for my own life
   What about you my dear friend?

7. Every day, I call on the Holy Family
   And my hands are blessed with gifts
   What about you my dear friend?

(5) Holy Family, The Joy of the World (Christmas Carol)

CHORUS:
Holy Family, the joy of the world
With virtues far enough
To transform the world
To make it a better place
To stay each day and night
Help us to honour you
Time without number
Forever A-A-A-Amen

1. Jesus, Mary and Joseph
   Yours was a perfect family
   To demonstrate to the world
   How to live a happy, modest life
   A life without sin but full of joy

2. Jesus, Mary and Joseph
   You brought light to the world
   To save each and every one of us
   From the darkness of sin
   And to make us live a joyful world

3. Jesus, Mary and Joseph
   Your virtues are light of the world

To make us model our own life
Like yours, which brings joy
And so, make us a joyful people

4. Jesus, Mary and Joseph
   Your virtues cannot be compared
   For they make us grow in holiness
   As well as revive our drooping spirit
   And so make us a holy people

5. Jesus, Mary and Joseph
   You care for my father
   You care for my mother
   And You care for children like me
   And You make us all a joyful people

Appendix C
PHOTOGRAPHIC SECTION
Activities of the Osundes with Pope John Paul II (canonised as Saint),
Pope Benedict XVI (Emeritus), Pope Francis, Apostolic Nuncios in Nigeria
and some Nigerian Catholic Bishops at different local and international
events, all aimed at building and promoting the Catholic faith

Above: Members of the Holy Family Society at a Mass in Abuja, Nigeria.

Left: The Apostolic Nuncio to Nigeria, Archbishop Antonio G. Filipazzi, seen here with Sir David E. Osunde when he visited the site of the Holy Family Society Pilgimage Centre in Abuja.

Below: Young seminarians who are members of the Holy Family Society expertly playing violin and flute at the society's ceremony in Abuja.

In the following pictures: the amazing, profitable and spiritual experiences of the Holy Family Society members who went to Mamfe Diocese in Cameroon, 16–22 August, 2013, to present the family spirituality programmes of the society to the worshipping community, priests and Bishops of the Bamenda Province.

In the following photos: delegates from Nigeria and members of the Holy Family Society at the World Meeting of Families in Dublin, Ireland, in 2018.

In the following photos: the City of Brotherly Love, Philadelphia, in USA, hosted participants with joy at the World Meeting of Families in 2015. The events at the international gathering were rounded up with a visit by Pope Francis.

Above: Members of the Pontifical Council for the Family who attended the World Meeting of Families in Philadelphia in 2015.

Right: Dame Mary-Joan Osunde, wife of Sir David E. Osunde, and Johnette B. Williams, a regular Anchor of the Women of Grace programme on EWTN.

Below: Three Bishops from Nigeria, namely: Archbishop Valerian Okeke of the Archdiocese of Onitsha (left), Archbishop Augustine Akubeze of the Archdiocese of Benin City (at the Centre), who is also the President of the Catholic Bishops' Conference of Nigeria (CBCN); and Bishop Martin Uzoukwu of the Diocese of Minna (right), with the Osundes in Philadelphia at the 2015 WMOF.

Bibliography

EWTN, 'Bl Luigi Beltrame Quattrocchi and Bl Maria Corsini', https://www.ewtn.com/catholicism/library/bl-luigi-beltrame-quattrocchi-and-bl-maria-corsini-5630; accessed 19 September 2021

LinkedIn, https://www.linkedin.com; accessed on 15 September 2021

Ott, M., *The Catholic Encyclopedia*, Vol. 8, 'St Isidore the Labourer', New York: Robert Appleton Company, http://www.newadvent.org/cathen/08189a.htm; accessed 19 Sept 2021

Pope Francis, Encyclical Letter *Fratelli Tutti*, Vatican, 2020

Pope Francis, General Audience 19 September 2018, Vatican

Pope Francis, Post-Synodal Apostolic Exhortation *Amoris Laetitia*, Vatican, 2016

Pope John Paul II, Apostolic Exhortation *Familiaris Consortio*, Vatican, 1981

Pope John Paul II, Post-Synodal Apostolic Exhortation *Ecclesia in Africa*, Vatican, 1995

Pope Paul VI, Dogmatic Constitution on Divine Revelation *Dei Verbum*, Vatican, 1965

Pope Paul VI, Pastoral Constitution on the Church in the Modern World *Gaudium et Spes*, Vatican, 1965

Stravinskas, P., *Catholic World Report*, '"All the way to Heaven is Heaven": 7 basic steps to holiness', https://www.catholicworldreport.com/2017/11/29/all-the-way-to-heaven-is-heaven-7-basic-steps-to-holiness/; accessed on 23 November 2021

The Holy Bible, Revised Standard Version, 2nd Catholic edn

Vatican Archive, *Catechism of the Catholic Church*, https://www.vatican.va/archive/ENG0015/_INDEX.HTM; accessed on 9 August 2021

Grandparents and parents, know that it is your innate responsibility to bring your loved ones under the protective canopy of Jesus, Mary and Joseph, the Model Family for the world, and you will remain eternally grateful to God, if you do. As you lovingly take this message to heart and share same to grandparents and parents who cross your path, this author is wishing you and your loved ones as well as all grandparents and parents God's infinite love and overwhelming spiritual care for taking positive steps to bring your own families under the ever growing, protective canopy of the Holy Family of Nazareth.